Proficiency in
Course
Key

Ona Low

Edward Arnold

© Ona Low 1986

First published in Great Britain 1973 by
Edward Arnold (Publishers) Ltd,
41 Bedford Square, London WC1B 3DQ

Edward Arnold (Australia) Pty Ltd,
80 Waverley Road, Caulfield East,
Victoria 3145, Australia

Second edition 1977
Reprinted five times
Revised edition 1986

British Library Cataloguing in Publication Data

Low, Ona
    Proficiency in English course.——Rev. ed.
    Key
    1. English language——Text-books for
    foreign speakers   2. English language——
    Text-books for foreigners
    I. Title   II. Low, Ona. New Certificate of
    Proficiency English course, with practice
    and test papers
    428.2'4   PE1128

ISBN 0-7131-8258-X

By the same author
Proficiency in English Course
Proficiency in English Practice, and KEY and CASSETTE
First Certificate in English Course, and KEY
First Certificate in English Practice, and KEY and CASSETTE
Speak English Fluently: Book 1
Speak English Fluently: Book 2

Text set in 9/10pt English Times Compugraphic
by Colset Private Limited, Singapore
Printed in Great Britain by Billings & Sons Ltd, Worcester.

1

Reading, vocabulary and comprehension

Metaphors (page 12)

Slumbered suggests that the hotels have been unimaginative and unaware of changes.

Acid — something extremely bitter and burning, like the guards' comment.

A football crowd is often made up of many thousands of people all walking to or from the match. The Oxford Street crowd is very large and moves in a similar fashion.

A magnet draws things towards itself as London does.

Word distinctions (page 12)

(a) plodded (b) ambled (c) tramped (d) strutted
(e) strolled (sauntered) (f) sauntered (strolled) (g) strode
(h) walked

Explaining the meaning of words and phrases (page 13)

(a) people providing accommodation and entertainment for guests
(b) describes objects and forms of behaviour that have existed for many generations
(c) the provision of somewhere to sleep and eat
(d) cannot be dealt with satisfactorily
(e) very large numbers
(f) costing more than they can afford
(g) see momentarily
(h) moves together as a large mass
(i) people living in Britain away from London
(j) impossible to provide
(k) find special enjoyment in

Short answers of one sentence (page 13)

1 Until a short time ago, the British travelled in other countries but had few visitors in their own; nowadays however many more tourists are arriving in Britain.
2 The nation's economy benefits from the money they bring.
3 The hotels and restaurants may be old-fashioned and inefficient.
4 The influx of foreign tourists is such a recent development that the tourist industry is only just becoming adjusted to the idea.
5 They are very high.
6 There are not enough hotels and those that exist are too expensive.
7 There are too many people watching and most of them see very little.

8 People should be hurried round in groups in a fixed time.
9 The street itself and also the shops are far too crowded by visitors.
10 It is implied that London is so crowded that the tourist has not enough space even to move his arms properly or to take a deep breath.

Longer answers to questions (page 14)

1 He may be dissatisfied by the low standards of restaurant meals. In addition he may well find that far too many other people are trying to enjoy such colourful ceremonies as the Changing of the Guard or to visit famous historical buildings. Oxford Street with its shops is usually crammed with other tourists. (*53 words*)

2 A suggestion has been made that the ceremony of the Changing of the Guard could be repeated during the day but the guards themselves have proved uncooperative. An idea has been mooted of hurrying people in groups through important historical buildings in a fixed time to relieve congestion. In order to spread the crowds, the beauty and absorbing history of other towns and regions have been given publicity but the short-stay visitor from afar who will not return prefers to concentrate his interest on London. (*85 words*)

Language practice
Grammar

A Collective nouns (page 14)

1 a choir — singers; a gang — criminals; a constellation — stars; an archipelago — islands; a staff — teachers, employees; a navy — ships; a fleet — ships, buses, taxis; a mob — disorderly people; a procession — people walking in an organised way; a congregation — people in church; an orchard — fruit trees; a family — related living things or languages; a board — directors; a brood — birds; a team — people playing or working in association; a jury — people listening to and giving a verdict on a court case; a cluster — flowers, fruits, people, houses, jewels etc.; a catalogue — names, book titles, things for sale etc.; a convoy — ships moving together for protection; a bunch — flowers, grapes, keys etc.; an anthology — poems; an audience — listeners; a swarm — insects; a crew — people operating a ship or a bus; a suite — furniture, rooms, related musical compositions; a herd — cattle, deer and some other animals; a grove — trees; a copse — trees; a bench — magistrates; a squadron — aeroplanes; a bundle — clothes, sticks, odds and ends; a pack — cards, wolves, dogs; a flock — sheep, birds.

2 1 is 2 are, their, pens, their 3 was, it, was 4 it, is (they, are — also possible) 5 are, their, they 6 is, it, was 7 are, their, heads, they, disapprove 8 has, it, is (have, they, are — also possible)

B Abstract nouns (page 15)

1   1 ambition, religion, oblivion, caution, rebellion
    2 rejection, contraction, intention, extension
    3 concentration, deliberation, emancipation, accommodation, execution
    4 condemnation, resignation, preparation, confirmation
    5 repetition, inhibition, extradition
    6 satisfaction, purification, rectification
    7 extinction, distinction
    8 resolution, revolution, absolution
    9 accession, concession, recession, procession
   10 ambiguity, incongruity, contiguity, assiduity
   11 generosity, pomposity, atrocity
   12 transparency, delinquency, efficiency
   13 visibility, audibility, legibility, eligibility, credibility
   14 glory, luxury, fury
   15 honesty, modesty, difficulty
   16 conformity, infirmity, extremity, insanity
   17 punctuality, equality, legality, stupidity
   18 poverty, humility, orthodoxy
   19 attainment, achievement, contentment
   20 acceptance, perseverance, resistance, arrogance, extravagance, brilliance
   21 violence, indifference, independence
   22 beauty, respect, delight, conceit, thrift, charm
   23 criticism, magnetism, heroism, dogmatism, Catholicism, Liberalism, Protestantism
   24 boyhood, knighthood, priesthood
   25 wisdom, boredom, freedom
   26 gratitude, solitude, aptitude, ineptitude
   27 laziness, tidiness, prettiness, loveliness
   28 gentleness, tenderness, eagerness, helplessness
   29 anger, hunger
   30 pride, hatred, pathos, virtue
   (Reference should be made to a dictionary for meanings.)

2   preference preferment;   conference conferment;   success succession successor;   pretence pretender pretension;   manhood manliness; attendance attention attentiveness,   admittance admission;   remittance remission;   tolerance toleration;   desperation despair;   friendship friendliness;   application applicant applicability appliance (Reference should be made to a dictionary for meanings.)

C A note on possessive forms (page 16)

(a) The second sentence means 'one of his sisters'.
(b) The second phrase means 'one of my uncles'.
(c) The second phrase means 'one of their cottages'.

Punctuation

A Full stop (page 16)

The following examples are phrases, not sentences, but they could easily be extended into sentences. In that case the full form is usual.

1 5 c.cs of water
a journey of one km.
six ft. tall
8 oz. of flour
one cwt. of coal
John Brown and Co. Ltd.
a B.Sc. qualification (Bachelor of Science)
cereals, e.g. wheat and rice
1900 A.D.
provisions for the journey: sandwiches, fruit etc.
Adam Atkins, M.P. for Churchdown West
our local magistrate, Henry Fielding, J.P.
an early departure at 5 a.m.
'a city corroded' cf. the poet's earlier reference to 'a city of tarnished silver'

the V.I.P. lounge at Heathrow Airport
4 Greenford Gdns.
the R. Avon at Stratford
the various Celtic languages i.e. Cornish, Welsh, Gaelic, Manx and Erse
research carried out when preparing a Ph.D. thesis
the Mt. Snowdon railway
a room temperature of 20°C.
achieve the V.C. for exceptional bravery (the Victoria Cross)
the M6 motorway
the A40 trunk road
the date MDCLXVI, carved above the porch in the year of the Fire of London.

2 1 Toilet requisites including soaps, cosmetics and combs, as well as . . .
2 A self-employed worker, such as a shopkeeper, . . .
3 Close . . . conferred, that is to say, a father, . . .
4 He . . . at half past ten in the morning and left at four o'clock in the afternoon.

3 FLAT TO LET: Self-contained. First floor. One reception room; one bedroom; kitchen and bathroom. Balcony. All modern conveniences. Central heating. Cold and hot water. All electric. Excellent cooking facilities. Garage available. Twenty minutes from Victoria Station. £120 per week inclusive. Telephone 19283 after 6.30.

B Semi-colon and colon (page 16)

1 breath;   2 post: 3 erratic: 4 neither required   5 animals:
6 defined;   7 smoking:

Word order (page 17)

1 The patient explained his symptoms to his doctor.
2 You must say good morning to him.

4

3 The reporter dared to ask the actress her age.
4 I think she told him a lie.
5 He gave his grandmother the mini-skirt.
6 May I offer you a cigar?
7 She will bring some fish for the cat and some bones for the dog.
8 He described to his wife the way he planned to decorate the room.
9 The scientist expressed his doubts to us.

Composition

Phrases and clauses (page 18)

(a) phrase   (b) phrase   (c) clause   (d) phrase   (e) phrase
(f) clause   (g) clause ('It is' is understood)   (h) phrase   (i) phrase
(j) clause   (k) clause   (l) phrase   (m) phrase   (n) phrase
(o) phrase   (p) phrase   (q) clause

Subordinate and main clauses (page 19)

(a) He has read the book which . . .
(b) Having . . ., he left.
(c) Did you sunbathe when . . .?
(d) They saw you when . . .
(e) unchanged
(f) unchanged
(g) The building should be safe in . . .
(h) I have invited Mary, who . . .
(i) He is unpopular because . . .
(j) Nobody knows what . . .
(k) They took torches so . . .
(l) I often forget where . . .
(m) You must remember when . . .
(n) He moved forward in order . . .

Examination practice

Reading comprehension, Section A (page 21)

1C   2D   3D   4D   5C   6D   7B   8C   9C   10A

Reading comprehension, Section B (page 23)

1B   2C   3C   4C   5B   6D

Use of English (pages 24-25)

1   1 cold/bad/unpleasant   2 spending   3 over   4 a   5 up
   6 borrow   7 against   8 at   9 agreed   10 give/pay
   11 information   12 journey   13 take   14 leave   15 least
   16 as   17 in   18 yourselves   19 staying   20 on

2   1 . . . first time he had (ever) been on board a ship.
   2 . . . the radio news was being read, he kept making angry comments.
   3 . . . you to become an engineer.
   4 . . . our taking some flowers to Aunt Penelope.
   5 . . . has had his car stolen.
   6 . . . he grows, the more cheerful he becomes.
   7 . . . to make it look more conspicuous.
   8 . . . far is it to the nearest post office?' she asked a policeman.
   9 . . . noisily than he needed (to)/than he need have.
   10 . . . that you may use the school library.

General practice (page 25)

1 His failure to complete the course spoilt his chances of promotion.
2 His repeated criticism of the plan exasperated everybody.
3 The public's enthusiastic reception of the news surprised no one.
4 His signing of his father's name on a cheque was regarded as forgery.
5 The party's attempt to seize power by force resulted in disaster.
6 The Government's second devaluation of the pound caused a new monetary crisis.
7 The workers' dissatisfaction with the new wage rates has led to a strike threat.
8 My friend's fierce attack on his previously held convictions left me speechless.

2

Reading, vocabulary and comprehension

Word distinctions (page 27)

(a) reduce   (b) declining   (c) lessened   (d) diminishing
(e) decrease   (f) deteriorate   (g) dwindled

Explaining the meaning of words and phrases (page 28)

(a) made longer   (b) a hotel sitting-room   (c) a small open space surrounded by buildings   (d) lower prices   (e) of the usual type and therefore lacking originality and imagination   (f) representatives who go from place to place to promote and record orders for their firms' goods

Short answers of one or two sentences (page 28)

1   The rooms at the front would be affected by traffic noise.
2   It is more than two hundred and seventy-five years old.
3   Service would cover the transport of luggage to rooms and the serving of food in the restaurant.
4   This might induce guests to prolong their stay and bed linen and towels would not have to be laundered so often.
5   Local residents might be attracted to these rooms and return frequently if they are pleasant and visitors might spend more money there if the appearance is congenial.
6   The food might be uninteresting and the service slow and unprofessional.
7   There would be a demand then for the rooms from business people, who would be paying the full rates.
8   The hotel is reasonably near the Cathedral and stands in the principal shopping street of the town.

Longer answers (page 28)

Notes only are suggested:
2   Proximity to the Cathedral. The historical appeal of the hotel. The traditional lounge and dining-room. The lift. The television in the lounge. The modern attractive bar.

3   Its position may make it noisy. Inadequate parking space. Old-fashioned furniture in bedrooms. Small dark lounge with inescapable television. Poor service and uninteresting food.

Language practice
Grammar

A   Uncountable and countable nouns (page 30)

1   Only the changed forms are shown, except where other words identify these.

(a) Their . . . mountains . . . their surroundings . . . remote countrysides . . . .
(b) The residents . . . their houses. . . . rods . . . they decided . . . .
(c) . . . profits . . . .
(d) They have . . . the weeks' . . . . Now they have . . . their correspondence.

(e) . . . our aunts . . . their flats . . . . They paid . . . they had saved for their old age.

(f) . . . daughters . . . their dark hair.

(g) The youths make . . . their parents' friends. . . . gives them . . . to their parents.

(h) . . . foods are (possible change but singular is more likely).

(i) Those shops sell . . . serve . . . teas. Can we get drinks there now?

2 (a) He was wearing a strange garment . . . for him.

(b) His earnings . . . and he has . . . .

(c) All his . . . of a torn-up newspaper . . . basket . . . carpet.

(d) . . . firm . . . agreement . . . a change . . . .

(e) He was lost . . . . the cow on the side of the dyke was . . . creature . . . .

(f) His business . . . he became a person . . . . his great riches, he gave . . . the benefactor . . . to his welfare.

3 (a) The pupils were clearly expecting something interesting to happen.

(b) behave in a way others expect of you; behave unexpectedly.

(c) He is a doctor or solicitor there; When used it is unsatisfactory; Not having done it for some time, he does something badly.

(d) in a newspaper; writing opposed to practical work; a game in which a runner lays a paper trail for others to follow; a book with a firm paper cover as opposed to a hard cover.

(e) in chains or fetters; tinned and similar preserved food carried by soldiers, explorers etc.; iron shaped by being run into a mould; device for smoothing clothes; iron parts of a structure; a factory for smelting iron or making iron goods.

(f) by physical compulsion; in operation (a law may be in force); come into operation.

(g) ruling a nation; no longer ruling; a building producing electricity; atomic energy; policy of a country attempting to coerce other countries by military strength; He is no longer able to speak; when he was in his most dominant position.

(h) too heavy; too light; get heavier; get lighter; heavier than allowed; a person employed to ensure that right quantities of goods are sold to the public; a person trained to lift heavy weights as a form of sport; a boxer of the heaviest category.

(i) a theatrical or similar presentation, whose proceeds are given to a good cause.

(j) scientific investigations of outer space; heating designed to warm a considerable area; visit at carefully arranged intervals; write as far as the bottom of the page.

(k) an extra bus; money collected for the victims of a disaster; a map showing heights of land.

(l) a feeling that danger is near; an awareness of things that is not conveyed through the normal five senses; to have meaning; in one way you are right; act sensibly after behaving foolishly.

(m) he is alert, ready to act and not easily deceived; power to react to a situation speedily; He is famous for his quick, clever humour.

(n) accept something on someone's word without proof; keep something safe, usually for someone too young to do this for himself; combinations of firms formed for their mutual advantage, who may control prices and production.

(o) manufacture of goods in very large quantities by specially controlled methods; making of more goods than can be disposed of.

(p) pay import tax; do what one ought to do.

(q) the various procedures that have to be observed when importing or exporting.

(r) a situation in which one's support is expected for conflicting interests.

(s) as decreed by Parliament; a sister's husband, or husband or wife's brother; begin to study to become a lawyer; the maintenance of good quiet behaviour among citizens disobeying the rules of the State.

(t) the ability to make friends; creative interests such as painting or constructional hobbies; having the quality of imagination and a high standard of achievement; imitative and not genuine; cunning.

(u) burning; being shot at; a group organised to extinguish fires; a portable device for putting out fires; an arrangement which guarantees to make good damage caused by fire if regular small payments have been inaugurated.

(v) drive faster than the law allows; a track for fast driving; a very fast motor-boat; a device for showing speed.

(w) concrete strengthened with iron or steel bars; a suggestion whose nature is clearly defined.

(x) a coin-operated device indicating how long a vehicle has been parked; disregard of parking regulations.

(y) an institution providing lessons by post.

(z) not working; occupations for free time.

4 The expression preceded by the article is dealt with first.

(a) period of low business and trade activity / low spirits
(b) many patients or clients / repetition to produce improvement
(c) a clever amusing person / clever amusing remarks
(d) a device for smoothing clothes / metal
(e) a formal address / the ability to speak and speaking properly
(f) the charge of a church parish / making his home
(g) an arrangement / a command / quiet controlled group behaviour
(h) a combination of business organisations / confidence
(i) an object for determining the degree of heaviness / got thinner and lighter
(j) any gas / coal gas
(k) percentage paid to author on proceeds from book or play / a member of the royal family
(l) a small glass ball / stone used in construction
(m) something that happens to us / knowledge gained from doing things
(n) one light / light in general

B The form and use of the passive (page 32)

1 (a) An extra large refrigerator has been installed so that the additional supplies of food that will be needed now can be kept fresh.

(b) Only by the use of the beauty soap now being introduced can the flawless complexion that is admired by everyone be ensured.

9

(c) By early September the harvest will have been completed and the corn stored in barns so that it can be threshed.

(d) When it was realised that a new motorway was being constructed through the housing estate, a petition against it was sent to the Ministry of Transport by the residents.

(e) The safe has been so designed that it can be opened only if a concealed electric switch has already been pressed.

(f) After the ship has been towed into the dock, she will be thoroughly overhauled, her state-rooms and cabins redecorated and new navigational equipment will be installed on the bridge.

(g) No one was taken in. In fact no notice was taken of what was said.

(h) A final date has been decided on by which it is expected that advantage will have been taken of the council's offer and the necessary equipment installed in everyone's house.

(i) Throughout the week-end the countryside had been lashed by gales. Corn in the fields had been flattened, trees blown down and roofs ripped off, and stories were being circulated of ships that had been driven aground and wrecked by the gales.

(j) He was hated by everyone. Not only were the local people forced to work throughout the long hours of daylight and even summoned at nightfall to his castle when extra servants were needed for the banquets that were given, but it was even decided whom they should be married to and every part of their lives was controlled by him.

2   Only words essential to an understanding of the answers are shown.

It has been reported by the Press that a series . . . thefts have been committed in . . . England. A large . . . area have been cut down and taken away. What . . . happening has been discovered by the local inhabitants only recently as the woods are not often visited in winter but it is thought that a considerable period may have been covered by the thefts as several districts have been affected. The trees have been cut down in . . . where no noise . . . lorries could have been heard. It cannot be explained why the trees have been taken or what will be done with them. Alcohol can be extracted from certain . . . but the possible . . . distillery can hardly be taken seriously. Is a hidden village sanctuary being constructed by these secret marauders in . . . cupboards? Are blocks of wood being surreptitiously sold to the local country people, whose time, like that of their German counterparts, is now being secretly devoted to . . . clocks? Or have the activities of the early charcoal-burners been resumed in these aged woods by their ghosts, unaware . . . atoms? It is said that watch is being kept by the police . . . wardens so . . . later the odd . . . trees will be explained unromantically.

4   (a) The B.B.C. have broadcast a message in which they have asked a certain Mr. Green, who, they think, is on holiday in Scotland, to go to the Overhill Hospital where doctors are treating his wife after a severe stroke.

(b) If the students have given sufficient time and attention to their work, they can take down passages in shorthand at 60 words a minute and can type letters quickly, neatly and accurately. They will have acquired some knowledge of book-keeping and office practice and they should have increased their command of English considerably.

(c) People in every town were celebrating Christmas. Delighted children were admiring Christmas trees, which busy mothers had decorated earlier. Tinsel adorned the branches while each member of the family had placed parcels beneath the tree. Outside, icicles festooned the roofs and snow covered the ground thickly while the wind was still tossing flurries of whirling flakes.

Punctuation

The apostrophe (page 34)

he'll be here soon; at four o'clock; the fisherman's rod; you mayn't stay; children's games; buy it at the bookseller's; she's away; people's homes; teachers' representatives; they'd be pleased to go; the actress's daughter; the bank manager's umbrella; they're away; John Davis'(s) horse; ten years' work.

Word order (page 34)

(a) I wonder what the driver of that car now racing along the wrong side of the road thinks he is doing.
(b) Coming home late last night a little drunk, he fell headlong into the ditch.
(c) As the furry caterpillar slowly crawled along the leaf the small girl screamed in terror.
(d) Why did the cook not tell me that this morning?
(e) Some students very much enjoy arguing with one another excitedly in gloomy cafés.
(f) He told me that on his first visit to London he had arrived at Victoria at exactly four minutes past four on the 4th April 1944.
(g) During his holiday in Ireland he sent some embroidered linen handkerchiefs to his mother by registered post.
(h) When he had to go to work at six o'clock, her husband always left the house very quietly so as not to disturb the rest of the family who were still sleeping soundly upstairs.
(i) The Duchess has often been seen in the market early in the morning carefully choosing vegetables.

Composition

Joining sentences (page 36)

(a) but   (b) colon   (c) so   (d) and, but   (e) and, but   (f) and, or, but   (g) and, but   (h) or, but, for   (i) but   (j) but, and

Subordinating conjunctions (page 37)

(a) as (when, after, because) (b) while (although) (c) When (As)
(d) Because (As, When, Whenever) (e) until (f) Unless
(g) Provided that (If) (h) provided that (if)

Examination practice

Reading comprehension, Section A (page 41)

1B 2D 3D 4A 5D 6A 7B 8B 9B 10B

Reading comprehension, Section B (page 42)

1D 2B 3A 4B 5A

General practice (page 43)

1 apologised for; referred to
2 succeed in; profit from/by; lose by
3 congratulated upon/on; pitied for; delighted about/at; envied for
4 objecting to; interfering with
5 contributes to; subscribes to
6 paying for; disposing of; saving up for
7 consists of
8 insists on; disapproves of; persists in; delights in
9 differs from; disagrees with
10 fight for/against; agree to; dissent from
11 warned about/against; punished for; advised against
12 depended on/upon; confessed to; specialised in

Reading aloud: practice passages (page 45)

1 A teacher is helping her foreign students to pronounce English sounds correctly.
2 A receptionist or sales person is taking down personal details of a potential customer in response to an inquiry.
3 A policeman or official is interviewing a suspect in a forgery case.

3

Reading, vocabulary and comprehension

Metaphors (page 49)

Two spectres etc. People regard the possible materialisation of these with fear and apprehension, and the two possibilities mentioned, though at present merely theoretical, have constantly worried (haunted) scientists. *To lay a ghost* is to cause it to disappear permanently and this has happened to one of the possibilities. The only defect of this metaphor is that ghosts are materialisations of people who have already existed: a future person or event has no ghost.

To loom is to appear indistinctly, often in a large and terrifying form. The exact nature of future possibilities is still uncertain, but the problem appears enormous and overpoweringly threatening.

A plague is a highly infectious disease which causes very great suffering and discomfort and is difficult to get rid of. Smog is not infectious but it certainly causes great discomfort and is difficult to disperse. There is a suggestion here of frequent repetition, not implicit in the original meaning.

Word distinctions (page 50)

(a) transfer   (b) carry   (c) transport/convey   (d) transmit
(e) convey
(a) dreary   (b) gloomy   (c) dismal   (d) squalid   (e) sordid
(f) shabby, drab   (g) dowdy

Explaining the meaning of words and phrases (page 50)

(a) that the problem caused by aerosols is the more important
(b) those who wish to preserve the life, beauty and amenities of nature
(c) possible future
(d) interfering with
(e) scattered
(f) increases
(g) the existing finely-adjusted relationship between
(h) without anything to prevent this
(i) keep within certain limits.

Short answers to questions (page 50)

1   The article refers to the building up of a layer of aerosols surrounding the earth.
2   As they are attached to the United States' space flight centre, they have ample opportunities for studying the effects of industrial waste on the atmosphere.

3 Gaseous waste products are being expelled in enormous quantities into the atmosphere.
4 It will take thousands of years for the effects of increasing carbon dioxide in the atmosphere to produce a change.
5 The aerosol layer causes the heat of the sun to be reflected back instead of allowing it free passage to the earth's surface.
6 There is a precise adjustment between the amount of solar heat taken in by the earth and the amount that is radiated back.
7 A large proportion of the light of the sun will never reach the earth but infra-red heat given off by the earth will be allowed to escape freely.
8 The ice would act as a mirror, sending back the sun's heat even if the aerosol layer no longer existed.
9 If atomic power could be developed soon enough, the amount of atmospheric aerosols need not become dangerous as the materials producing them would no longer be used.

Longer answers to questions (page 51)

1 Cumulative amounts of carbon dioxide in the atmosphere may result in higher temperatures. The intensification of atmospheric aerosol pollution, caused by the discharge of gaseous waste from factories, could form a layer excluding sunlight but permitting the loss of earth heat, thereby lowering temperatures. (*44 words*)

2 Aerosols, which are minute solid or liquid dust fragments, congregate in the atmosphere into a screen round the earth. This deflects the light and heat received from the sun but at the same time can be easily penetrated by heat radiated from the earth so that this escapes. Temperatures will gradually fall and the polar ice region will extend considerably. The beginning of a new ice age in little more than fifty years seems quite possible. The ice would reflect away sunlight even if the aerosol layer ceased to exist. (*90 words*)

Language practice
Grammar

Definite and indefinite articles (page 51)

1 Only those words preceded by an article are shown.

(a) a practice,   the suburbs,   the county town
(b) the sun,   the rain,   the country,   the enjoyment,   a holiday,
    the weather
(c) a drink,   the café,   the corner,   the one,   the back,
    the Town Hall
(d) the children,   the men,   the classroom,   the school,   a film,
    the children
(e) the Thames,   the Cotswolds,   the North Sea
(f) the statesman,   an expert,   'The Times',   'The Economist',
    the library,   the House of Commons,   a note,   the important news,
    the day,   the latest information,   the international situation

14

(g) the mystery
(h) a solicitor, the law, the truth, the dispute, a letter, the people
(i) an accident, the Great North Road, the other day,
a sports model, the other, a saloon, another, the others
(j) a Thursday, the twenty-sixth, a national holiday, a lot,
an enjoyable time, the weather
(k) the Isle of Man, an island, the Irish Sea

2 The noun preceded by the article is dealt with first in each case.

(a) the news that was received; some news
(b) certain known luggage; some pieces of luggage
(c) washing the clothes; washing oneself; a short time; almost no
time
(d) a Doctor Sykes — it is possible I know him; the Doctor Sykes —
the well-known one; Doctor Sykes — the doctor with this name
(e) the most important — no other is so important; a most — a very
(f) the head postmaster — defining which James Jones; a head
postmaster — this is his job; Head Postmaster — stating his title
(g) it was not printed again; a week ago
(h) visiting there; as a prisoner
(i) a special formal celebration; a certain meal
(j) a week — in a week's time; the week — not at the weekend
(k) place of business; in a public position of authority
(l) on the blackboard; on the ship
(m) in the answer — the one answer sent; in an answer — more than
one answer has been sent; in answer — in reply to
(n) a factory/a lake — one of various possibilities;
the factory/the lake — both are known, possibly the only ones
(o) farming; no longer at sea.

3 (a) 'one' stresses the fact that there is only one
(b) the chest — the large box; his chest — part of his body
(c) blackcurrant jam — not anything else; some — a certain amount of
(d) the building; the art of film-making
(e) the amount she buys; the unit of weight according to which she buys
(f) a different job or routine; change — excess payment that is returned
(g) cake — not anything different; some — a piece; a — a small cake
(h) Nature — plant and animal life; human nature — what
characterises people as distinct from animals.

4 (a) Coal is a dark, . . . matter, and used as fuel. A coal-mine is a deep
pit . . . coal is excavated. A coal-miner is a worker in a coal-mine. A
coal-field is an area where coal is mined. A coal-merchant is a
tradesman who supplies coal to the consumer.
(b) Information is knowledge about a certain subject supplied by an
apparent authority on the subject.
(c) A fine is money paid as a form of punishment for a minor offence
against the law or the regulations governing the community.
(d) A charge is: (i) an energetic forward movement of an attacker
against an opponent. (ii) a sum . . . (iii) an amount . . .
a gun . . . . (iv) a task, a duty, a responsibility.
(v) an accusation against a possible offender.

Punctuation

Capital letters (page 53)

(a) He lives in Beech Street . . . River Ash . . . Oakchester Station.
(b) As . . . Swiss Tourist Office . . . French, Italian, German and English . . . English Channel.
(c) He . . . B.Sc. . . . Economics . . . Scottish . . . Marketham Post Office.
(d) On . . . Tuesday . . . February . . . History of Civilisation . . . Christmas . . . .
(e) The Member of Parliament for Elmers Bank . . . If . . . 'The Times' . . . B.B.C. . . . I . . . .

Word order (page 53)

1 (a) Never in his life had he worked so hard.
 (b) Hardly was Mr Littlejohn inside . . . .
 (c) Not until then did she realise . . . .
 (d) . . . . So do their wives.
 (e) Rarely do we have such . . . .
 (f) Only in an election year do most politicians . . . .
 (g) Only after he had read the newspaper . . . . did he realise the danger . . . .

2 (a) He has ordered a dictionary as he wants to improve his spelling.
 (b) The fact that the aspidistra near the window keeps out the light annoys me.
 (c) The guide was showing the tourists the prehistoric carvings with . . . .
 (d) He speaks only his own language.
 (e) In the market place I bought some fish which smells atrocious.
 (f) The judges will examine the flowers in . . . .
 (g) He eats hardly anything.
 (h) Astronomers have detected several moons . . . .
 (i) It . . . . read in newspapers about the new fashions.
 (j) The director said he earned barely enough . . . .
 (k) He . . . . horse without a head had . . . .
 (l) Your prize can be either . . . .

3 (a) The postman usually comes much earlier.
 (b) Normally he does not speak politely.
 (c) Emphasis is laid on his refusal to speak before.
 (d) Emphasis is laid on how fast she moved.
 (e) Emphasis is laid on the fact that there will not be a long wait for this.
 (f) And not to someone else?.
 (g) This will quite certainly happen.

(h) The chaos was quite unprecedented.

(i) But most of the time I am not interested.

Choice of expression

Common grammatical and structural faults (page 54)

1 It is advisable to buy a ticket in advance as it may be found that all seats have been taken and it will be necessary to stand.

2 As we live in . . . to us.

3 The mist . . . fell. As it was only . . . afraid, so she . . . basket and left the house. After only a few yards the mist swallowed her up. As she felt her way along the fence, a twig lashed her face. Then she heard . . . her. She stopped and they stopped: she hurried forward and they pursued. She was at the mercy of a panic . . . world.

4 Edinburgh . . . city which has . . . events. Mary, . . . Palace and Bonny . . . there.

5 Many . . . restaurants especially in cheerful and friendly ones, for there they can . . . surroundings.

6 The next . . . property, which proved to be a huge . . . house standing in . . . neglected. As they approached . . . renovate the house.

7 He left . . . that he would be spending . . . York.

8 As several . . . had had to close down, there was . . . areas. There was also redundancy . . . works.

9 It is a horrifying experience to awaken . . . cellar.

10 It is said that he very much enjoys letter-writing.

11 He very much likes . . . wine.

Composition

Writing sentences (page 55)

1 While I was exploring the garden, I came across a shaded pool with water-lilies floating upon it and gold and black fish moving . . . .

2 It must be admitted that the English . . . changeable so that people . . . them, but this variable weather has the one advantage of providing an infallible . . . .

3 In the sixteenth . . . England and so it is difficult to understand why there were . . . centuries though it is generally accepted that British . . . .

4 At six o'clock in the evening, when a dog ran straight in front of a car it narrowly . . . over as the driver braked sharply.

5 The clerk whom you saw last week has lost his job as he was lazy and inefficient and was often late arriving but Mr Cooper . . . .

6 If you are a good boy and we are able . . . notice, you may be taken to the circus where you will see . . . elephants much cleverer . . . zoo.

Examination practice

Reading comprehension, Section A (page 61)

1B 2C 3A 4A 5C 6B 7C 8C 9C 10C

Use of English, Section A (page 61)

1 1 has been working / must have been working   2 unless
3 thinking / feeling   4 however   5 shall spend
6 have been cut   7 to waking / getting up   8 such a noise /
so much noise   9 have burned (burnt) / have got burned
10 them singing

2 1 I missed seeing the carnival procession this year.
2 He should have worn thicker clothes.
3 He agreed to my publishing (my publication of) his memoirs.
He agreed to let me (to allow me to) publish his memoirs.
He agreed that I should publish his memoirs.
4 He suggested my returning (that I should return) home as soon as
possible.
5 They greeted each other when they met.
6 I am postponing (shall postpone / have postponed) my journey to
Paris till(until) next Monday.
7 He might not have heard what you said.
8 He spends most of the day working in his garden.
9 He told me what his flat was like.
10 A knock at the door prevented my answering (prevented me from
answering) his question.

Use of English, Section B (page 63)

1 It is normally assumed that it is easier to be tidy when there is plenty of
storage space and yet it is when they are restricted to a small space that
people have to be most tidy.
2 In a theatre and a television studio, preparations for a performance are
carried out in apparent confusion and similarly a Chinese woodcarver
works in the confusion of busy streets.
3 Possible storage space may have been utilised in creating a larger living-
room, and at least the fact that there is nowhere to keep things
discourages the hoarding of non-essentials.
4 The person who has charge of the house may prefer untidy surroundings.
5 Father plays golf and the family uses the luggage when going on
holiday. Presumably there is a baby for the perambulator and slightly
older children who play with the plastic toys. The family enjoys sitting
in the garden in the deck-chairs and perhaps having tea round the fire
from the trolley. A middle-class family that appreciates comfort is
suggested.
6 'It would be proved from case-histories and depth interviews.' The book
would deal with some aspect of either sociology or psychology.
7 In the order in which they are normally arranged.
8 It would appear to mean 'designed to fit into the shape of a ship'.
9 'that they work only in clean and meticulously orderly surroundings'.

10 A genuinely tidy person puts things in their right places automatically whereas an untidy one has to make an occasional and not always successful effort to do this.

11 The deck-chairs and the bulkier plastic toys may, like the things already mentioned, also be homeless.

12 'Chronic' refers to an illness from which a person suffers continually and similarly the tidiness will continually recur. The destruction must be 'ruthless', that is to say, without any mercy or softening of heart.

13 Everything may have been put out of sight but the insides of cupboards and drawers may be far from tidy.

14 Many workmen can achieve satisfactory production only when their tools are systematically arranged. Other craftsmen, however, work purposefully in surrounding confusion, and back-stage chaos seems inseparable from theatrical and television performances. *(31 words)*

15 Tidiness, that is to say putting things away neatly and where they are readily be found again, is facilitated where there is plenty of storage-space. On the other hand a very restricted living or working area may enforce the return of everything to its only available home. In this case, the restriction of one's possessions to essentials can assist in achieving neatness. In essence, however, tidiness is a quality which depends on individual temperament and training, which determine whether things are returned to their right places automatically or only with considerable effort and will-power. *(94 words)*

General practice (page 64)

1 (a) I like it.   (b) Yes, I'm afraid so.   (c) Well, I want to.
   (d) Yes, I think so.   (e) Yes, I see.   (f) Yes, I believe so.
   (g) No, I hope not.   (h) Yes, I suppose so.   (i) Yes, I regret it.
   (j) Yes, I know.   (k) No, I don't think so.   (l) Well, I wonder.

2 (a) Have you ever seen a brown-eyed cat?
   (b) A hawk is keen-sighted.
   (c) He is a very self-assured young man.
   (d) A square is a four-sided geometrical figure.
   (e) She bought a sixty-watt light bulb.
   (f) He is a ten-year-old chess master.
   (g) Accidents are less common in well-lit streets.
   (h) She is a cashier in a self-service restaurant.
   (i) This house is crammed with labour saving equipment.
   (j) I have found my long-lost dictionary.

3 1 (b) He struggled remarkably courageously.
     (c) His struggle was remarkably courageous.
   2 (b) He moved unexpectedly quickly.
     (c) His movement was unexpectedly quick/fast.
   3 (b) The boxer punched extraordinarily strongly.
     (c) The boxer's punch was extraordinarily strong.
   4 (a) The expert predicted with amazing accuracy.
     (c) The expert's prediction was amazingly accurate.
   5 (a) The surveyor measured with very great care.
     (c) The surveyor's measurement was very careful.
   6 (a) He behaved with absurd formality.
     (b) He behaved absurdly formally.

4

Reading, vocabulary and comprehension

Metaphors (page 69)

Colour is identified with interesting change, and there is little of this in his life.
Dream refers to the day-dream of a delightful future that most people enjoy.
A *drug* may offer a pleasant escape from harsh reality, and if it is *non-toxic*, it will have no harmful after-effects.
If *unbalanced*, he will no longer behave in a stable way, taking various needs and interests into account, but may develop unnatural obsessions.
Feverish suggests illness with a high temperature, something of an abnormality.

Word distinctions (page 70)

1 A destination is a place to which one is going.
2 (a) crave for   (b) yearn for   (c) long for   (d) desire   (e) want
3 In meaning (small / time unit) and pronunciation (maɪnjúːt / mínɪt).
4 Few = too few. A few = some.
5 A customer buys something, usually from a shop.
7 (a) steal   (b) burgle   (c) rob   (d) plundered   (e) looted

Spellings (page 70)

(a) immediately   (b) phenomenon   (c) deterioration
(d) maintenance   (e) acquirement   (f) obsession
(g) exhilaration   (h) exaggerated   (i) irreparable
(j) conscience   (k) psychological

Explaining the meaning of words and phrases (page 70)

(a) the unforeseeable results
(b) given him a far wider range of opportunities
(c) he was more likely than not to succeed
(d) weakness
(e) the unexpected winning of a large sum of money may cause anyone without a strong character to behave foolishly
(f) laws designed to suppress it
(g) a possibly harmful means of psychological escape from a monotonous life.

Short answers of one or two sentences (page 71)

1 A man building a house may be involved in any one of a number of accidents.
2 Despite the various risks involved in the average day's existence, most

people survive unharmed for many years, and new things are constantly being achieved.

3 Besides unconsciously gambling against destiny, men could consciously gamble with one another for things they owned.

4 While not necessarily involving any great loss, gambling can add excitement to a dull existence and thus keep people cheerful and hopeful.

5 Gains achieved by gambling depend on luck and not on honest work.

6 Gambling has a fascination for him, with never-fading hopes of success and the occasional delight of winning.

7 His earnings could be given not to him but his wife, to spend on the family.

8 Various criminal groups would offer opportunities for illicit gambling and this would involve far worse abuses.

9 The government could pass laws to restrict the enormous profits made by large-scale promoters of gambling.

Longer answers (page 71)

1 Unless it was otherwise decided, when individuals gambled among themselves, the chances were equal for all the participants and whatever was staked was available only to them. In large-scale commercial gambling, the chances that any one individual will win are very slight but the promoters benefit enormously, often with little fear of losing themselves. (*54 words*)

2 The victim himself becomes completely addicted to gambling, which deprives him of his possessions, his sense of his own value and decency and his judgment of right and wrong. He cannot be cured because he has no wish to be and he will stop at nothing to get money. His family live in poverty and endure the depressing sight of his demoralisation, without sharing his delight at his occasional frantically welcomed gains. (*72 words*)

3 Commercial motives for encouraging gambling can be minimised by governmental restrictions on the profits derived from it. The gambler's family would suffer less if his earnings were paid direct to his wife. A thorough investigation into the nature of this obsession is needed. The long-term solution lies in an education designed to encourage hobbies and an outlook that needs no harmful distractions to combat boredom. (*65 words*)

Language practice
Grammar

A Pronouns (page 71)

1 (a) The clerk told his friend that his boss, though inefficient himself, was always referring to the clerk's lack of qualifications. The speaker wondered why he himself had been appointed.

(b) A man . . . street which was crowded . . . *Or*: the train crowded with holidaymakers was preceded along the quayside street by . . . flag.

(c) He says . . . from the farm near which he has rented a caravan.

(d) The oven was already very hot, so after ten minutes I was able to eat the pie which I had put in to warm.

(e) The clock which stands on the mantlepiece has to be wound up twice a day as it is very old.

(f) The people questioned by B.B.C. interviewers in the streets are sometimes indignant.

(g) In the centre of the table stood an Italian rose bowl which she . . . .

2 (a) People who hate crowds keep away from those seaside places which, on a fine summer Bank holiday, are so crammed with people and cars that there is almost no space to sit down.

(b) Many . . . festivities and usually get good prices for the birds. Sometimes however a surplus may cause prices to fall considerably and some turkeys even remain unsold. In this case much of the trouble taken and food bought are wasted.

(c) The children were throwing stones and watching the ripples which these caused spreading over the lake surface. By lifting momentarily the dead leaves, like tiny . . . boats, the ripples gave the impression . . . .

(d) Meaning may be completely altered by the intonation with which ideas are expressed. An unconscious abruptness which may offend people can result not from the words used but from the fact that the rise and fall of the voice . . . meaning. It is advisable to accustom the ear to . . . meaning that can be given . . . intonation.

(e) Milk, which is essential for children, is in short supply and so unfortunately must be imported. As it can be obtained . . . way off, there will be difficulty in organising the necessary special transport service.

3 (a) . . . counting them, an operation which happens . . . .

(b) in the fog, a mishap which could have . . . .

(c) A body has been found near the sea, a discovery which . . . .

(d) . . . in 1066, a date which everybody remembers.

4 (a) one (you), long(s);   one's (your);   one (you);   one's (your)

(b) whom;   who   (c) they do   (d) All I said (All that I)

(e) whom   (f) It is said   (g) into its sty   (h) who have;

their opinions   (i) as we have (as us)   (j) whose horse.

5 (a) Hamlet, which . . . ways,

(b) captain, whom . . . bridge,

(c) student who / that

(d) recipe (that / which)

(e) Shropshire, which . . . poems,

(f) most (that)

(g) The car (which / that) Or: in which they are travelling

(h) countryside, which . . . heed, . . . any that grow

(i) His grandmother, whom he . . . to, Or: to whom . . . money,

(j) mouse that / which . . . house that / which

(k) The girl (whom / that)

(l) revue, whose author . . . anonymous, Or: the author of which

B Pronouns and adjectives (page 74)

1 (a) some kind of job / the kind of job does not matter if it provides experience
   (b) a person / who she is does not matter provided she is quiet and tidy
   (c) in one place / everywhere
   (d) a suggestion (probably you would) / a question (the answer is unknown)
   (e) with difficulty / not properly, untidily
   (f) expected answer 'yes' / answer unknown
   (g) how much and what kind / which of a known group
   (h) he has eaten something / he has almost no appetite
   (i) criticism of the small number is implied / a small number of
   (j) she would choose her guests carefully / she had very few guests
   (k) talk when they are alone / talk to other dumb people
   (l) the fastest car / faster than the other two
   (m) nobody / they choose employees carefully
   (n) a certain amount of work (unstressed) / but there is very much more to be done.

2 (a) wants his; he hands his   (b) intends, its   (c) was   (d) he has
   (e) everybody has   (f) everything

3 (a) . . . several large fish.   (b) . . . such white washing.
   (c) . . . a lot of . . .   (d) . . . fluffy; the others . . .
   (e) She has few . . .   (f) Aeroplanes like those . . . Or: That kind of aeroplane is . . .   (g) How handsome he is!

4 (a) whatever   (b) wherever   (c) however   (d) whoever
   (e) whichever   (f) whenever

C Adjectives (page 76)

1 treacherous, courageous, fiery, apparent, reversible, Parliamentary, Governmental, consultative, revolutionary, humorous, intermittent, impulsive, monotonous, enthusiastic, adventurous, planetary, scientific, sympathetic, elusive, circular, apologetic, energetic, apathetic, decorative, experimental, titular, muscular, angular, mountainous, watery, wintry, bookish, obligatory, geometrical, acceptable, inventive, ingenious, infantile, idiotic, absorbent, dictatorial.

2 These word groups could form part of sentences:

the earthy smell of potatoes;   earthly possessions (contrasted with spiritual);   earthen pots
brass candlesticks;   a brassy clang; brazen impudence
childish fits of temper;   childlike innocence;
young children;   a youthful figure
a graceful dancer;   a gracious smile
old books;   an elderly solicitor;   in olden times
human needs;   the humane treatment of animals
a wood fire;   a wooden floor;   a wooded hill-slope

gold coins;   golden hair
sunny weather;   the solar system
glass vases;   a glassy stare;   a glazed door
a hearty appetite;   heartfelt sympathy.

3   The same applies here:

a bright light;   a light punishment
a fit of coughing;   fit again after an illness
a cold in the head;   cold weather
a tribal chief;   the chief industries
a college principal;   the principal subjects
a walk across the common;   common interests
Trafalgar Square;   a square room
a spinning top;   a mountain top;   the top class
bacon fat;   a fat dog
a glass of stout (beer);   a stout man.

4   The same applies here:

prize cattle;   a correspondence course;   Brussels lace;   a garden path;
a stamp collection;   evening dress;   a bargain basement;   a toy train;
a china cup;   a tape measure.

5   superficial (shallow);   lunar;   nocturnal;   insular (narrow-minded);
mental;   nasal;   ocular;   aural;   manual;   dorsal;   dental;
oral (spoken);   temporal (temporary = for a short time);   mural;
marine;   pensive (thoughtful);   legal.

6   tolerant = open-minded;   tolerable = bearable
trustworthy = reliable;   trustful = without suspicion;
trusty (old use) = faithful
confident = sure;   confidential = secret
selective = subject to choice;   select = distinguished
appreciative = admiring;   appreciable = considerable
nightly = every night;   nocturnal = by night
powerful = strong;   powerless = unable to act
nervous = from the nerves / afraid
nervy = easily agitated
gassy = effervescent;   gaseous = consisting of gas
pitiful = causing pity (also: piteous);   pitiable = worthy of pity;
pitiless = without pity
eventual = final;   eventful = with many things happening
effectual = removing all difficulties;   effective = producing a result
dependable = reliable;   dependent = needing support from someone
comprehensive = inclusive;   comprehensible = can be understood
flowery = over-decorated (language);   floral = of flowers
luxurious = richly comfortable;   luxuriant = plentiful
brotherly = as felt by brothers;   fraternal = linked by common ties
fatherly = kindly and protective;   paternal = having the
characteristics of a father
motherly = kind and sympathetic;   maternal = of a mother

continual = recurring over a period; continuous = unbroken over a period

forceful = masterful and energetic; forcible = by force

nebulous = unsubstantial; nebular = of a large star group

starry = shining like stars; stellar = of stars

handy = accessible; manual = operated by hand

lawful = allowed by law; legal = connected with the law

picturesque = having the prettiness of a picture; pictorial = having the characteristics of a picture.

7 widely-read; highly-esteemed; carefully-planned; highly-organised; brightly-lit; strongly-criticised; well-made; much-needed; brightly-coloured; long-awaited. (There are other possibilities.)

8 (a) this was still happening / they were already assembled
  (b) the prisoner was being watched / he was watching
  (c) the man behind / in front
  (d) getting ripe / already ripe
  (e) they had come there for shelter / the trees protected them
  (f) the men talking / being talked about
  (g) it is starting now / it is already being run
  (h) the man is showing reverence / others are reverencing him
  (i) the writer is criticising / is being criticised.

9 (a) so conservative as (b) more reserved than (c) more powerful than (d) more tiring than (e) the first (f) heavier than (g) so useful as (h) more graceful than (i) worth more than (j) as long, as (k) the most influential

10 (a) When she is depressed, a new hat will make my mother feel happier.
   (b) As he was loaded . . . .
   (c) In my opinion as a married man, my . . . .
   (d) He was so completely carried . . . his enthusiasm, that every obstacle . . . .
   (e) There seemed . . . explorer, who had been deserted by his guide, would find . . . .
   (f) He was racing . . . hour when an old man . . . .

Punctuation

Commas (page 78)

1 . . . matter, he said, . . . it,' and added, . . .
2 . . . and, if it's true, . . .
3 The rain, . . . morning, . . .
4 . . . mantelpiece, . . .?
5 . . . and, as . . . answer, . . .
6 No commas.
7 Sandra, . . .? Yes, . . . kitchen, . . . matches, a pipe, three letters, . . . book, . . .

Choice of expression

Written as distinct from spoken forms (page 78)

1 . . . could not. . . .
2 John Keats wrote many beautiful poems.
3 There is often considerable unemployment in the shipbuilding industry.
4 . . . own two cars . . . luxuries, which may include a television, . . . and electric blankets.
5 I was alarmed by an ear-splitting shriek which broke the silence.
6 . . . ten o'clock in the evening . . . six o'clock in the morning.
7 Among the considerable disadvantages which many au pair girls have to work under are too little free time, . . . English and spoilt . . . to manage.
8 She had what might be described as a menagerie in her house, with five dogs, three cats, two canaries, five rabbits and five adopted children. It was very kind of her to have accepted so much responsibility, but we felt she had undertaken too much.

Spelling aids (page 79)

labelled labelling; wrapped wrapping wrapper; disappeared disappearing disappearance; sadder saddest sadden; shipped shipping shipment; remitted remitting remittance; slimmer slimmest slimming; installed installing installation instalment; stopped stopping stopper; concealed concealing concealment; transferred transferring transference; benefited benefiting; knitted knitting knitter; commoner commonest; preferred preferring preferment preference; inner inmost inward; happened happening; quarrelled quarrelling quarrelsome; deferred deferring deferment deferential.

Composition

Loose, periodic and mixed sentences (page 80)

One example only is given in each case.

1 (a) *The actress posed for photographers with her tame cheetah*, as she hoped to create for herself an image of fierce unpredictable beauty but the normally docile animal demonstrated its unpredictability by leaping towards the photographers, who abandoned their cameras and fled.

2 (a) Foreigners often have an erroneous impression of other cultures and at the same time may tend to overrate simplicity of style when reading

another language, so that the authors most esteemed overseas may be less popular at home and in fact *many writers are better-known abroad than in their own country.*

3 (a) He had been so absorbed in exploring the cave that he did not notice *that he had been trapped by the tide* and now he was faced with the unpleasant prospect of spending at least six hours in this dark and clammy sea-guarded dungeon.

Examination practice

Reading comprehension, Section A (page 88)

1B   2D   3D   4D   5D   6A   7D   8A   9B   10C

Reading comprehension, Section B (page 89)

1C   2A   3B   4B   5D   6C

Use of English, Section A (page 91)

1   I had difficulty in seeing the ship as it was so far off.
2   This was the first time I had used a typewriter.
3   Only by using my torch could I see my way.
4   He said that his absence from the concert had been the result of a severe headache.
5   "What a wonderful afternoon!" she exclaimed / said.
6   He apologised for not having written to me the previous week / the week before.
7   "Whose turn is it?" the teacher asked.
8   "It would have been better for you to have typed . . ." (better if you'd typed)

5

Reading, vocabulary and comprehension

Metaphors (page 97)

soaks The colour is represented as a liquid which all objects absorb and then display.

royal richly-coloured, especially with purple, crimson and gold

embroidery forming a picture apparently made with coloured silks or wools

Valkyrie These battle maidens rode furiously across the sky, possibly screaming.

raise rolling mountains The wind causes the sea to rise, forming very high waves.

brittle silver sword-points pierce the night-velvet The stars appear no larger than points, apparently cutting through the smooth dark sky — they seem hard and brilliant like shining metal that could easily snap.

thread The branches resemble strands of fibre stretched against the sky.

glimmers... night Winter suggests darkness and spring the dawn, but this is still far distant so its light is very faint.

Word distinctions (page 97)

Examples of usage, not sentences, shown.

(a) Almost interchangeable with the meaning of sharply painful or sorrowful: poignant / bitter memories, regrets, grief, disillusionment. But: bitter hatred, quarrels, hardships, flavours.

(b) *burst* a balloon, a tyre; *break* a cup, a bone, a promise.

(c) *florid* complexion / decoration (bright or too elaborate); *floral* patterns = based on flowers.

(d) *surfeited* with rich food = having had too much; *satisfied* = having had enough, or contented: *satisfied* with life.

(e) *success* = opposite to 'failure'; *succession* = sequence, one after the other: a succession of misfortunes.

(f) *chilly* = lacking warmth unpleasantly; *cool* = lacking warmth pleasantly: a chilly Autumn evening; a cool shady garden (But: a chilly or cool greeting).

(g) *current* = defined movement of air or water; *currant* = a small fruit.

(h) *purple* grapes; *crimson* roses.

(i) a *mood* of depression, cheerfulness, irritability, friendliness etc; a *temper* = restricted to a good or bad temper (amiability or the reverse).

(j) *strip* = a narrow piece of something; *stripe* = a band of colour across a surface.

(k) *delusive* = giving a false impression; *illusory* = existing only in the imagination.

(l) *audacious* means daring (opposite: timid); *self-effacing* means the opposite.

(m) Vapour which *condenses* into water becomes more compact, hence the second meaning of 'become smaller and more compact'.

Spellings (page 98)

wrath, wrapping, wraith
wren, wrestle, wretched, wreath, wrench, wreck
wriggle, wring, writhe, wrinkle, wrist
wrought, wrong

Explaining the meaning of words and phrases (page 98)

(a) energetic in a rough way, usually from high spirits
(b) curled up and withered from dryness
(c) the pleasures of summer that are so abundant and rich that one can tire of them
(d) become warm, rich and sweet
(e) is very richly coloured
(f) a quiet and sad morning, on which outlines are made indefinite by mist and with a peacefulness which induces thought
(g) large and rounded like big waves
(h) make their bodies as small as possible while the wind blows out their feathers
(i) be as good as hoped for.

Short answers to questions (page 98)

1 To an optimist, spring promises a wonderful future summer but the writer has doubts about the glories both of spring and summer.
2 They are brightly-coloured, erect and appear to be unafraid of anything.
3 Autumn is the season when the heat of summer is mitigated by the colder air of approaching winter.
4 The colours of spring, whether bright or pale, are simple and plain; autumn colours are a mixture of many shades and are softer and richer.
5 The trees suggest woodland, while arable, pastoral and moorland are also described.
6 The clouds are dispersing so that the sun breaks through.
7 This is suggested by the description of a lamplit room with a fire, hot toast, records of quiet or imaginative music and plenty of enjoyable books.
8 Animals must die so that other younger ones may take their places, thus ensuring continued new life
9 The real spring will bring unpleasant weather and the tiredness that people suffer after enduring the winter, unlike the ideal spring of glorious weather that we envisage.

Longer answers (page 98)

1 Spring suggests exaggeration and wild energy that is soon exhausted. The gay flowers soon die and serve as a depressing reminder of the impermanence of youth and beauty. The weather may be cold, wet and windy and people are possibly too tired and listless after the winter to enjoy themselves. (*50 words*)

29

2 (*Notes only*) Peaceful sunlit warmth / quiet misty mornings and evenings / bracing and refreshing days when summer heat is cooled by the chill of coming winter / fierce noisy winds that denude trees and cause storms at sea / prolonged gentle rain / early frosts / increasingly cold winds with the approach of winter. (*47 words*)

3 The weather, often warm and sunny, is sometimes dimmed by mists. Colours are less bright and hard but richer and there is the quiet satisfaction of ripe fruit and a harvest safely gathered. Darker evenings are spent indoors in lamplight and firelight with the enjoyment of music and books. Sleep and dreams are pleasanter. There is more time for reflection and awareness. The only disturbance is the occasional stormy winds and the only sadness the consciousness of the dying year. (*80 words*)

Language practice
Grammar

A Present and past tenses (page 99)

1 Only the verb tense and explanation is suggested.

(a) They have (habitual)   (b) They spend (habitual)   (c) It starts (future expressed by the Present Simple)   (d) I am working (arranged future)   (e) I have visited (a past action that may be repeated in the future)   (f) I have been studying (a period which extends till now)   (g) I go (habitual)   (h) I am learning (action extending through now)   (i) I have read (recent past time extending till now)   (j) I have been learning (as (f))   (k) I have been living (same)   (l) He teaches (habitual)   (m) They are always changing (repeated action with some slight irritation)   (n) They have been discussing (as (f))   (o) It is being held (arranged future)   (p) It is made (habitual)   (q) Financial problems have been dealt with (period of time including the present)   (r) . . . have been introduced (recently).

2 (a) He is probably still there. He has returned from there.
   (b) As = while. As = because.
   (c) An action. A position.
   (d) The second suggests some annoyance.
   (e) Once. Several times.
   (f) He no longer paints. He still paints.
   (g) The lesson is still continuing or has only just finished. The lesson has quite definitely finished.
   (h) He was still there. He was no longer there.
   (i) Future work. Work already completed.
   (j) After they changed. He was already in the road.
   (k) At some previous time. Immediately before.
   (l) The journey was made. The journey was arranged.
   (m) She was out. She was intending to do this.
   (n) It was with the repairer. It was in good condition again.

B All tenses (page 100)

1   The tenses are made clear by the questions and explanations can be found in the reference material on tenses.

2   (a)   A weekly arrangement. Probably only on the following Thursday.
    (b)   It is now about midday. It is now afternoon or evening.
    (c)   They would like to know when this will happen. They are surprised when it happens. They will be surprised when it happens.
    (d)   The walk had finished or was almost finished. It was happening just then.
    (e)   Expresses surprise or annoyance. All his letters are extraordinary.
    (f) The report is finished. It may or may not be finished.
    (g)   I interrupted him. The speech followed the question.
    (h)   They will be in the class before they take it. It will be taken before they enter.
    (i)   at that time; at some time previously; until that time or very recently; in the future; he was willing to work there.
    (j) Expresses annoyance. This is a normal arrangement.
    (k)   She never comes on this day. She will not come on this occasion. She refuses to come.
    (l)   It was his habit to do this. A promise to do this in the future.
    (m) It was his habit. He was annoyed about this.
    (n)   He will start then. It will have been finished then.
    (o)   A future arrangement. He is there now.

3   had arrived, had been reserved, had signed, paused (the Past Perfect in this and several later examples would be more logical but the shorter Past Simple forms are more likely to be used)
    Have any letters arrived
    am ('m), had ('d) forgotten, arrived
    gave, had obviously been delivered, wondered, had written, stuck
    may, asked
    have already gone, said
    have ('ve) been travelling, have not (haven't) eaten, complained, am ('m)
    will be coming (is coming), told, I'll be making (I'm making), Shall I make
    I'd be
    I'll see, are, I'll bring, will you be leaving (are you leaving), Shall I ask
    think, I'll sleep, got, was catching, I'm always travelling, I'm, will do (would do)
    rang, had signed, appeared, led, had put, was just leaving, paused
    hope, you'll have (have), said
    was thinking, was preparing, should (would) have expected, would sleep
    was washing, brought, knew, would not keep, drank, was not leaving (would not be leaving), had, had had, would be, had
    fell, had got, was dreaming, was running, was disturbed, was, seemed, was howling,
    stated (had stated), were not allowed
    had not unpacked, pulled, did, felt, had forgotten, opened, read
    shall claim, have taken (took)
    was, had been, had gambled, had been imprisoned, drowned (had been drowned), had been left

was howling (howled), remembered, had died
threw, ran, was, went, could see, was, closed.

Punctuation

Inverted commas (page 103)

1 (a) said, 'Yes, . . . yesterday,' and . . . added, 'or . . . yesterday?'
   (b) . . . asked, 'Has anyone telephoned?' (New P.) 'Yes,' said his wife,
       'a man . . . again.' (New P.) 'I wonder . . . been,' speculated . . . .
   (c) 'Shall we have a drink in "The Red Lion"?' Peter suggested. 'I want
       . . . play "Only Death is Endless".'
   (d) . . . papers: 'The . . . eye.'
   (e) When I say 'three', all . . . .
   (f) . . . word 'self-seeking' rather than 'selfish'.
   (g) 'Many . . . work,' and 'Too . . . broth,' . . . co-operation.

Choice of expression

Choice of words (page 103)

1 a well-mannered boy; a warm sunny day; an enjoyable holiday;
   an interesting book; a rest in peaceful pleasant surroundings;
   a satisfying job; a sympathetic and capable teacher; appetising food;
   an enjoyable time; a beautifully-designed car; an exciting surprise;
   an imaginative cook; coffee with a pleasant flavour; warm sunny
   weather.

2 (a) I am very sorry to say that your usual room is not free now and the
       only one I can offer you is less comfortable.
   (b) During the nineteenth century most servants lived and worked in very
       unpleasant conditions.
   (c) Thank you for your letter of the 12th May.
   (d) The lambs playing in the meadows looked so delightful that we felt
       happy to be alive.
   (e) A fall in sales reflects public anxiety about the financial situation.
       Lower taxation would help to restore confidence and this would lead
       to increased production with the result that the threat of
       unemployment due to redundancy would be averted.

Reported speech

Statements (page 104)

1 (a) He complained that he was getting tired of waiting. He had been sitting there for half an hour. The same thing had happened when he had come there the previous day. The next time it happened he would report it.
   (b) My old friend suggested that it must have been at least ten years since he had last seen me.
   (c) The secretary commented that he had expected to see more people there that evening. The club should have publicised the meeting in the previous day's paper.
   (d) When my uncle advised me that I ought . . . get my weight down, and informed me that he had walked five miles a day when he had been my age, I reminded him that he was not me.
   (e) James told his wife that they would have to arrange their holiday during the coming week. They . . . month before.
   (f) The owner of the next flat told Henry that if he had to keep . . . foods, he really ought . . . of his own.

2 (a) I knew he had telephoned an hour before. He had told me so himself.
   (b) I shouldn't have been surprised if you had had to pay duty on that.
   (c) It seemed very likely that even if he got a rise he would still give up his job.

Examination practice

Reading comprehension, Section A (page 108)

1B 2B 3C 4A 5D 6A 7C 8D 9D 10D

Reading comprehension, Section B (page 109)

First passage

1D (no actual apology made) 2C 3A (culminating in) 4A

Second passage

1A 2A 3C 4B

Third passage

1B 2A 3C 4D

General responses

1C 2A 3A 4C

Use of English, Section A (page 112)

1 reading/seeing   2 by   3 that   4 take   5 that   6 space
7 upon   8 quite/completely/utterly   9 are   10 more than/but
11 in   12 made   13 taking   14 of   15 of   16 with   17 of
18 other   19 besides   20 take

General practice (page 113)

1A   2B   3B   4B   5A   6B   7A   8B   9D   10A

Reading aloud (page 114)

1 A customer in a bookshop is asking a sales person for advice on how to
  obtain a particular book.
2 A politician is giving a speech on the merits of his party. He could be at a
  rally or in a television studio.
3 A choir master is practising a piece of music with his choir. They are
  likely to be in a church.
4 A woman is making an urgent telephone call to a plumber. She is at
  home and expecting guests for dinner.

6

Reading, vocabulary and comprehension

Word distinctions (page 118)

(a) join   (b) gather   (c) unite   (d) clustered   (e) meet   (f) links
(g) amalgamate   (h) assembles
(a) coaxing   (b) convinced   (c) urged   (d) persuaded   (e) wheedle

Explaining the meaning of words and phrases (page 119)

(a) money spent on paying people to do a job that will produce profit
(b) the many and various ways in which separate people or numbers of people
    working together have dealings with one another
(c) wasteful of money
(d) the possibility of being changed easily to suit varying conditions
(e) concern about how much will have to be paid as rent
(f) according to a rigid and formal pattern

(g) forcing its way in

(h) to modify their own wishes so as to fit in with what is best for everybody

Short answers to questions (page 119)

1 It can cause annoyance and hindrance to everybody and lower their standard of work.

2 The features of the building itself and the communications which must be available between people and groups must be taken into account.

3 An open-plan arrangement eliminates or considerably reduces the division of floor space into rooms and compartments and so affords more flexibility in the utilisation of the space available.

4 The minimum space has been utilised in order to economise on the rent payable and this has resulted in a rigid and probably cramped arrangement.

5 Some modern homes, hotel reception rooms, schools and museums make use of this system.

6 A considerable amount of noise, especially from people's voices, may cause disturbance.

7 Most higher ranking staff prefer their own room, which gives the effect of a secure, quiet, secluded world.

8 As the expertise for such conversion may not be available from the company staff, a highly-paid specialist may have to be consulted, who could suggest radical changes and reconstruction.

9 The external shape and construction of the building may be so designed as to promote the maximum efficiency and well-being of those working in it.

Longer answers (page 120)

1 (*Notes only*) Maximum utilisation of available floor space / provision for more efficient communications between individuals and groups working on related projects / greater ease in introducing changes in arrangement as these are required by new work schemes / creation of more congenial atmosphere. (*39 words*)

2 The main purpose of office planning is to minimise the time wasted in circulating and exchanging information and material. Staff are positioned according to the part they play in the general work scheme, so that groups which must communicate with one another frequently are close together. Some privacy is achieved by the use of movable screens and noise from other areas is reduced by various acoustic devices. The absence of walls allows for regrouping when a major change in organisation has to be introduced.
(*84 words*)

3 (*Notes only*) Senior members of the staff may dislike being deprived of their privacy. The available floor space may not be of a suitable shape. Measures must be taken to cut down disturbance from increased noise. The conversion itself may necessitate employment of a consultant who may suggest far too radical changes and charge a fee so high as to make the proposed changes uneconomic. (*62 words*)

Language practice
Grammar

Conditions (page 120)

1   Only a suitable subject and verb tense are suggested here.

(a) we should cause   (b) he concentrates   (c) food supplies could not have been brought   (d) they ate   (e) we should have been able to learn   (f) he had not been   (g) there would be   (h) speed limits are imposed   (i) there will have to be   (j) he had

2   Only a suitable subject and verb are suggested here.

(a) I should take   (b) I should have been working as   (c) They are
(d) I shall walk   (e) It would have been   (f) I should tell him
(g) I should talk about   (h) I should have liked   (i) It will have to provide   (j) I should not have met   (k) The harvest will be
(l) I should refuse   (m) I should introduce   (n) I should suggest
(o) It would have been

The imperative and subjunctive moods (page 121)

1 Let's sit down.   2 were   3 were   4 were   5 had murdered
6 lived   7 were (to be)   8 was   9 had   10 might help

Verbs used as auxiliaries (page 121)

1   an order was given; a statement was made
2   she did not telephone; she telephoned him
3   some determination or intention is expressed; an estimate of the time it will take
4   he no longer does this; he is accustomed to doing this
5   a statement; an order
6   this always happened; he is clearly not angry as this is not happening
7   this had been planned; this was happening
8   this was the arrangement; the arrangement did not come off

Notes on some modal verbs and on 'need' (page 121)

1   (a) had not been able   (b) had had to   (c) would have to
   (d) had been allowed   (e) have had to

2   (a) no   (b) no   (c) no   (d) yes   (e) no   (f) no   (g) yes
   (h) yes   (i) possibly   (j) no

Punctuation

Brackets and dashes (page 122)

1   not since — wait
2   flakes — all
3   ago — at
4   (David . . . down)
5   (previously . . . Empire)

The punctuation of letter headings and endings (page 122)

H. Lead, Esq.(,)
The Pressed Steel and Alloy Company(,)
19-31 Greatburn Street(,)
Crusham(,)
Lancs. 60V 4T9

Honeysuckle Cottage(,)
Fairview Gardens(,)
Sunnyvale(,)
Hants. HE2 34L

23rd February, 19-

H. Lead, Esq.(,)
The Pressed Steel and Alloy Company(,)
Crusham(,)
Lancs. 60V 4T9

Dear Mr Lead,

Yours sincerely,

(Mrs R. Feather)

Choice of expression

Choice of words (page 122)

1 Every year larger numbers of tourists make use of the country's overcrowded main roads and it seems very probable that before long there will be too many cars to cope with.

2 It was raining heavily. (*or*: It was pouring with rain).

3 I regard Kim Borg, the Finnish bass, as an outstandingly gifted singer.

4 He had an arresting face. Snow-white hair . . . brow;   keen blue eyes . . . aggressive nose overshadowed a weak receding mouth and chin.

5 We shall fight the decision with determination and shall do everything possible to ensure justice.

6 On a completely calm sea the boat rested motionless but he stood there with a white face wishing . . . .

7 (Avoidance of 'countryside' repetition) The countryside . . . noisy traffic there. New . . . disfiguring its quiet beauty.

Reported speech

Questions, commands, exclamations, special expressions, other points (page 123)

1 (a) He commented on the exhausting day he had had.
  (b) He expressed his annoyance.
  (c) He dismissed the idea sharply as nonsense.
  (d) He commented scathingly on the stupidity of what I had said.
  (e) He expressed surprise at the big teeth I had.
  (f) He showed concern at how ill I looked.

2 (a) Spot's master called him a good dog and said that there was a biscuit for him.
  (b) Eileen's friend commented admiringly on how beautiful Eileen looked.
  (c) He expressed his annoyance at having left his address-book at home.
  (d) The sergeant ordered the men to stand to attention and turn their eyes to the right.
  (e) She called him an idiot as he was sitting on the eggs.

3 (a) She told me that the liqueur chocolates were delicious and asked me whether I would like some.
  (b) He commented on how cold the day was and said that he needed warmer gloves.
  (c) She asked me when I had got back and whether I had enjoyed the journey.
  (d) The teacher told me to speak more slowly, adding that I would not make so many mistakes if I did.
  (e) Mother asked Jim if he would mind posting the air letter for her, and she told him not to forget it.

(f) My new friend said that if I needed help I could telephone her at the number she gave me.

(g) My neighbour suggested my having a cup of tea or, if I preferred it, coffee.

(h) Mr. Green asked his secretary whether she had a copy of that day's newspaper and told her to lend it to him when she had finished with it.

4 (a) Robert asked his landlady who lived in the . . . . She replied that nobody did at the moment. An elderly . . . who had had four boxer dogs, had lived there . . . months before, but he had died . . . inherit. lived . . . . Robert asked what had happened to the dogs.

(b) After settling . . . the stout lady asked the waitress for a pot of tea for two but her friend immediately made it clear that she did not want any as she no longer partook . . . . They were known to be bad for the heart. She asked the waitress whether she had any lemon juice and . . . . The stout lady expressed her impatience and asked whatever absurd fad her friend would adopt next, offering her some of the delicious chocolate cake. The friend was horrified at the idea of chocolate cake which she claimed was shocking for the digestion. She asked whether she might have a couple . . . . She assured her friend Clara that within a year Clara would be a martyr to gout, quite apart . . . . As she popped two . . . Clara stated that it was better to suffer . . . months.

(c) In an address to Parliament, the Member for South Northend declared that in addition his party intended to bring to the members' notice a grave scandal. All of them must know by that time that . . . erected the year before had been the lowest in the previous ten years. Yet two years before, the present Prime Minister had promised . . . completed. The Member challenged him to deny that statement. He asked the Prime Minister to explain why in that age . . . . He expressed doubts whether the Prime Minister's family had ever been forced . . . and demanded whether the less privileged of their society had to continue . . . . He stated that just two days before however he had been informed that plans existed for . . . party then controlling the Government. If these plans were accepted, the new building would cost . . . pounds. He informed the House that he would say no more.

(d) The television interviewer asked the famous producer what his next production would be. The latter   publicity. He said that they had been rehearsing . . . . 'She Stoops to Conquer' was coming . . . of that month . . . . When asked who would be taking the part of Candida he explained that the company had originally hoped . . . but, it would be remembered, she had been involved . . . weeks before. She was at that time convalescing in Switzerland. They had however discovered . . . O'Donovan. She had a warm . . . and had so . . . that he believed she would prove . . . Candidas they had ever seen.
     The interviewer asked whether the producer himself would be taking . . . .

He was informed that that would not happen on this occasion. The producer was doing some filming just then . . . and if he tried . . . he would wear himself out completely.

The interviewer thought he was right. He must . . . exhausted. He asked whether the producer's book of memoirs was completed.

He was told that it had been finished the previous month but the producer would be revising it in his spare moments. He would like . . . reference to the new production.

On behalf of all the listeners the interviewer asked whether he might wish him every success with his many new ventures. He thanked the producer for coming along that evening and said goodbye to him.

The producer said goodbye and expressed his appreciation of their chat.

(e) The young . . . screen.

He suggested that the viewers should examine a photograph. It was a picture . . . as she had been a month before. He asked whether the viewers saw the . . . and told them to look . . . . He could assure them . . . of the previous winter.

The week before Miss Maxim had started . . . . She had gently massaged . . . with the vitamin-charged skin food. They now had to meet . . . . The young man extolled her beauty. He told the viewers to observe in close-up the satin-soft . . . . Every line had been . . . . He asked them whether they wanted . . . and told them to buy . . . that very day. If they applied . . . days they would have . . . . He urged the investment of two pounds in beauty, in endowing their weather-tired skins . . . allure they . . . their skins could . . . .

Composition

Facts expressed in sentences: definitions (page 125)

A thermometer is an instrument for measuring temperatures.
Water is a liquid composed of two hydrogen molecules to one oxygen.
A passport is a document issued by the State which entitles the holder to visit other countries.
A handkerchief is a piece of material or paper used when blowing one's nose.
A triangle is a three-sided geometrical figure.
A loom is a structure on which cloth is woven.
A canal lock is a section of a waterway where boats can be raised or lowered to another level.
A mule is an animal whose parents are a horse and a donkey.
A prima donna is a leading woman opera singer.
A policeman is a man who has the job of enforcing the law.
A driving licence is a document which authorises the holder to drive a motor vehicle.

A convector heater is a space-heating device which produces warm air.
Wine is fermented grape juice.
Porridge is a food made from oatmeal cooked in water.
A wardrobe is a cupboard or enclosed space in which clothes are hung.
Obstinacy is a possibly illogical determination not to change one's mind.
A waiter is a restaurant employee who serves food and drinks at the tables.
Baking is a form of dry cooking in an oven.
A cinema is a building in which films are shown to the public.
Irrigation is the supplying of land with water by means of ditches.
A precipice is a very steep abrupt slope.
An electric torch is a portable battery-operated device for giving light.
A spanner is a tool with one or more jaws for turning screws.

Examination practice

Reading comprehension, Section A (page 136)

1A 2B 3D 4A 5A 6B 7D 8C 9D 10B

Use of English, Section A (page 137)

1   1 As he felt very tired . . . .
    2 As soon as (When) he heard . . . .
    3 . . . while I wondered what . . . .
    4 . . . as he had nowhere . . . .
    5 . . . where he opened a shop.
    6 . . . though I doubted whether . . . .
    7 . . . after they had taken.
    8 He worked so hard that he made . . . .

2   1 It was not until after the had posted the letter that he remembered
      . . . .
    2 This letter must have been posted weeks ago.
    3 You need not (needn't) have hurried so much.
    4 He convinced me of the necessity of making . . . . / He convinced me
      that I ought to (should) make . . . .
    5 I had never been to the restaurant when it had not been full . . . .
    6 Despite my efforts to understand . . . .
    7 His style demands the reader's intense concentration (to understand
      it).
    8 His frequent depression is due to (caused by) his inability to get about
      very much.
    9 Taking more exercise would keep you thinner / would help you to
      lose weight.
    10 In no way did my parents ever influence me.

Use of English, Section B (page 139)

1   In both periods it was a commercial centre. (*see line 8*)
2   Alfred the Great had earlier promoted learning there so that the town
    had become an important cultural centre.

3 It is a contrast between the noisy traffic-packed roads and the peaceful areas away from them.
4 This could be a respect for beauty in architecture.
5 The buildings are of a wide range of age and style so that the walker is constantly delighted by unexpected interesting things.
6 In its quietness, dignity and prosperity, it is typical of the countryside in which it stands.
7 It is equal to the interest of the cities named previously.
8 The words are not essential to the thought being expressed but are a half-humorous comment.
9 Many past 'visitors' came to subdue, rule or in some way make use of the city. Most of those who arrive today come to see and admire.
10 It emphasises the odd contrast between the Alfred who encouraged learning and the warrior depicted by the present statue.
11 It is large, high and far more impressive than anything round it.
12 in contrast to this noise
13 The word suggests purposeless hurrying.
14 the ways in which people view life and their surroundings.
15 with solidly-constructed straight roads radiating from it
16 capital
17 Winchester has many beautiful old buildings and also qualities of refinement, dignity and lively creativity which are all true aspects of the English heritage.
18 Winchester, at one time capital of England, has a long history dating back to pre-Roman times and specially associated with the important early English king, Alfred. Incorporating Norman and Gothic elements, its cathedral has both beauty and interest. The town has many houses of varying ages and styles, some built in early Elizabethan days. Winchester College, a famous public school, was founded in the fourteenth century. The visitor would enjoy the tranquillity of the Close and the quieter streets, the variety, dignity and inventiveness of much of the architecture and the respect for tradition and beauty which characterise the city. (*99 words*)

General practice (page 139)

1 They made him sing.
   They knew that he would sing.
   They wanted him to sing.
   They advised him to sing.
   They enjoyed his singing.
   They believed that he would sing.
   They saw him sing.
   They forced him to sing.
   They let him sing.
   They thought that he would sing.
   They realised that he would sing.
   They allowed him to sing.
   They appreciated his singing.
   They encouraged him to sing.
   They dreaded his singing.

2 1 once
2 the Fourth / the nineteenth
3 one twenty-three / the twenty-first / nineteen ninety-nine
4 a double
5 a single
6 three nil
7 forty love
8 the fifth / one hundred and twenty-three / Fourth / 0 nine eight seven
9 the eighth
10 three / triple
11 nine million four hundred and thirty-eight thousand three hundred and two
12 a (one) quarter / a (one) third / sixteen / an (one) eighth
13 point 0 four
14 fourteen pounds fifty-six pence
15 four / three / the fourth
16 ten / an eleventh

3 1 Phonetic pronunciation
2 A stress mark
3 Uncountable, Countable, plural, transitive verb
4 that is (Latin: id est)
5 They are all expressions containing the word defined.
6 Iron can be hammered into shape when it is hot. Make fullest use of an opportunity especially of influencing people.
More pieces of iron or iron tools heating than one can deal with — too many occupations and interests.
7 Creases in material are smoothed into non-existence when material is ironed.

4 1 I wonder if you'd mind helping me with this case?
2 Don't forget to write to me, will you.
3 Would you be able to change a ten-pound note for me?
4 I'm sure you'd like a cup of tea, wouldn't you?
5 Would you open this suitcase, please.
6 Would you be so kind as to (could you) tell me the way to the station.
7 You will remember to post that letter, won't you.
8 Would you like to read now.

5 H hesitation   C surprise   I challenge   D a pause for thought
A relief   E qualified approval   B agreement   F resignation
J decision   G ironic surprise

7

Reading, vocabulary and comprehension

Metaphors (page 145)

Hovering is maintaining a position a short distance above the ground — this would enable a sudden strike downward. Disagreements are poised, waiting at any moment to descend, that is to start.
A *barb* is a bent sharply pointed end which will penetrate and hold the victim. The news could be exchanged maliciously with the idea of hurting.
A *mask* hides the natural face. The correct behaviour soon fell away revealing their natural selves.
To *glow* is to give off heat and there is a possibility that flames could appear at any moment. The quarrels showed signs of revival.
To *clamour* here suggests to demand a hearing.
A *pounce* is a sudden jump on a victim with the intention of harming it.
Any sign of enjoyment would bring down a sudden intense feeling of guilt.
The *chill* combines a feeling of coldness (from the emptiness) and apprehension at the thought of death.
The *shadows* here are feelings of depression or sorrow and the occasions named do not cause any feelings of this kind.
Friction is rubbing, possibly causing discomfort. It refers here to the irritations resulting from meetings between members of a family.

Word distinctions (page 145)

1 (a) leading   (b) Bring   (c) conducted   (d) takes   (e) fetch

2 (a) outing   (b) voyage   (c) trip   (d) expedition   (e) excursion
   (f) journey

3 necessary; essential. Similar meanings to *essential*: indispensable (cannot be done without); vital (essential to life).

Additional word distinctions (page 146)

1 (a) darn   (b) mend   (c) reconstruct   (d) mend / repair
   (e) patch   (f) overhaul   (g) renovate

2 (a) assassinate   (b) execute   (c) sacrifice   (d) slaughter
   (e) massacre   (f) murder   (g) kill   (h) commit suicide

3 (a) insolvent   (b) insoluble

4 alternate;   alternative

5 industrial;   industrious

6 (a) recompense   (b) reward

Explaining the meaning of words and phrases (page 147)

(a) the blunt expression of opinion without any attempt at diplomacy and the ever-present possibility of quarrels.
(b) to give the impression of success and correct behaviour.
(c) anecdotes based on memories.
(d) established ceremonial procedure.
(e) made fun of in many countries and valued far below her true worth.

Short answers to questions (page 147)

1 Journeys were slow, uncomfortable and rarely undertaken except by people who had their own coaches.
2 People tried to show that they were rich, successful and respectable and knew how to dress, cook and entertain suitably.
3 Most of the conversation dealt uncharitably with the family news and scandal, with other relatives, memories and disagreements.
4 The memories were mainly of disagreements, jealousies and general hostility.
5 There was a feeling of annoyance, unfriendliness and considerable criticism, but in meeting one another, people felt they had done the right thing.
6 They can show off their new fashionable clothes, enjoy the food and drink, believe they are superior to others and generally feel at ease.
7 They behave very circumspectly, lowering their voices and treating the bereaved with a slightly condescending pity and concern.
8 This helps the guests to forget the recent funeral and their own future demise.
9 It will cease to exist and children will be brought up in large groups with no known relatives apart from their mother.

Longer answers (page 148)

1 At first participants were stiffly correct in behaviour, trying to give the impression of success and respectability. Gradually they showed their real characters, often unpleasant, and old enmities were revived. Most of the things said were unkind and there was little genuine friendliness. Children unwillingly encountered little-known cousins and were forced to show off their talents. (56 words)

2 (Notes only) Nowadays people have many more interesting ways of spending their time: outings in their car in summer and television and possibly a warmer and more comfortable home in winter. Fewer relatives because of smaller families and these few may be widely scattered. (42 words)

3 (Notes only) Wedding: opportunity for dressing up and enjoying good food and drink — special occasion for close relatives with more distant relatives and friends (less privileged) in background, but general feeling of cordiality. Funerals: carefully subdued formal behaviour with special consideration for bereaved — less solemnity during following meal but consciousness of own mortality.

Christenings, Christmases and twenty-first birthday celebrations probably most enjoyable and good-humoured. (*62 words*)

Language practice
Grammar

Verbal constructions (page 148)

1   1 in gardening; pottering about out of doors.
  2 visiting the museum; we should like to see the harbour.
  3 reading; to borrow it; for me to understand.
  4 to give the patients cigarettes; on bringing in packets.
  5 in isolating radium; to achieve this.
  6 from reaching the summit; to seeing the view.
  7 cleaning the house; having a cup of tea.
  8 standing in the rain; getting wet.
  9 of/about overtaking everything on the road; for speeding.
  10 the woman of failing to pay; get off the bus.
  11 arguing; making a decision.
  12 the men working; waiting.
  13 not come in; latecomers to disturb the lesson.
  14 whether the price is competitive; on our reviewing it.
  15 sulking; being given fish for breakfast.
  16 whitewashing the ceiling; to paint the woodwork.
  17 playing to learning; of having too much free time.
  18 take photographs here; being arrested.
  19 reading the forbidden book; to tell us what it was about.
  20 in learning to drive; to pass the test eventually.
  21 building their nests; how to construct them.
  22 having robbed the bank; to question him.
  23 to sleep out of doors; it will rain during the night.
  24 losing my temper; showing my true feelings.
  25 borrow my typewriter; to buy one of your own.
  26 for disturbing me; not to worry.
  27 interrupting; the speaker to admit he was lying; to leave; for disturbing the meeting with the truth.
  28 him to become an artist; him from giving up his studies; to postpone his decision.
  29 riding and driving through the countryside.
  30 me to buy her a hand-embroidered blouse; to look for one.
  31 taking these tablets; to take them regularly.

2   1 He is to study Mathematics.
    makes me study; lets me study; had better study.
  2 I happened to meet him.
    avoided meeting; postponed meeting; insisted on meeting.
  3 Do you dare to go home alone?
    mind going; persist in going; object to going.

46

4 He promised to calculate how much it might cost.
suggested calculating; is used to calculating; succeeded in calculating.
5 I should like to have played with trains as a child.
remember playing; deny having played; missed playing
6 He is learning to play chess.
knows how to play; spends time playing; would rather play.
7 The retired boxer means to buy a public house.
suggests buying; thinks he will buy; had better buy.
8 The harbour master thinks that the boat will arrive early.
wants the boat to arrive; will allow the boat to arrive; prefers the boat to arrive.
9 He has decided to eat a ham sandwich.
feels like eating; has finished eating; enjoys eating.
10 He seldom suggests sending news to his brother abroad.
fails to send; forgets to send; troubles to send.
11 I regret that I am late.
apologise for being; cannot help being; prefer to be.
12 I long to ski through the forest.
am looking forward to skiing; enjoy skiing; imagine myself skiing.

Punctuation

Hyphens (page 150)

coming-of-age
old-age
old age
bus stop
heat-resistant
underground
present-day
anti-vivisectionist
one-year-old
one year old
rarely occupied
thirty-two
mouth-organ
ex-president
three-sided
looking-glass
lighthouse
non-stop
anti-social
general hospital
medium-sized
all right
playwright
washing-up (*noun*)

roast beef
cat-burglar
many-coloured
department store
road junction
everyday
every day
hire-purchase
estate agent
football match
look-out
dairy-farming
highly-strung
public library
panic-stricken
starting-point
seaside resort
hard-boiled
grapefruit
hard-wearing
multi-storey car park
meanwhile
waterproof
midnight

Choice of expression

Sentence pattern (page 150)

1 The daily newspaper, which has become an essential part of our lives, appears indispensable. We owe a great debt to the people who established it.
2 (*First sentence unchanged*) The problem of providing adequate . . . generations is still unsolved and there is little time left to deal with it.
3 . . . case. She then discovered that by . . . ground.

Reported speech

Changing from reported to direct speech (page 151)

1 (a) 'Do be careful!' she implored them. 'Don't leave the mountain hut tomorrow if the weather gets worse.'
   (b) 'Would you please telephone me as soon as you get home,' he said.
   (c) 'I'll lend you the duplicator when I've finished with it,' I said.
   (d) 'What a beautiful miniature!' she exclaimed. 'I'd simply love to wear it.'
   (e) 'Those infernally noisy aeroplanes!' he grumbled. 'Something . . . them.'
   (f) 'If you'd asked my advice . . . car you were buying,' he said, 'I'd have recommended an estate car.'
   (g) 'What century would you like to have been born in?' he asked. 'Do you think you'd have been happier then?'

2 (a) 'What have you been doing for the past hour?' Mrs. M. asked her guests.
      'We just bought . . . then found a quiet cáfe,' they said. 'We've been planning the tour we'll be making next week.'
   (b) 'Don't speak so loudly,' he said. 'The . . . listening. What you just said is confidential.'
      'I was speaking in a whisper,' I said, 'and anyhow the chauffeur arrived . . . fortnight ago and can speak no English.'
      'You must . . . granted,' he replied.
   (c) 'Hey!' he shouted. 'Did you win yesterday's match?'
      'No, we didn't.'
      'What a pity!' he said. 'Better luck next time.'
   (d) The dealer . . . murmured, 'She'll sail . . . she'll do, like a dream.'
      'Birds don't sail and ninety miles an hour's a nightmare,' said . . . .
      'Look at these gadgets,' urged . . . dealer, indicating the . . . system.
      'I don't smoke,' stated the man, 'I'm stone deaf and I'm taking . . . Equator.'

'Just what sort of car are you looking for?' asked the dealer.
The man explained. 'I want one you can guarantee will get me . . .
down, that will carry my luggage, my dog and my wife . . . trails, that
will not deteriorate . . . storms and that will not cost . . . £1,500.'
The dealer . . . chrome. 'I can't help you,' he admitted. 'I should
try the garage round the corner if I were you. They have . . . stock.'

(e) I rang . . . given.
'Can I help you?' a girl asked.
'May I speak to George,' I said.
'Which George do you want? There are five Georges in the office.'
'I don't know his second name but he's got red hair.'
'That's George Murphy, the junior clerk,' the girl replied. 'What's
your name, please?'
When I told her, she said, 'Would you wait, please. I'll put you
through.'
'Well?' I heard George answer.
'Mr Marvin Newman would like to speak to you.'
George's tone changed immediately. 'Thank you very much,' he said
to the girl, and to me, 'Good morning, sir. George Murphy speaking.'
'Newnham here,' I replied. 'I hope I'm not disturbing you.'
'Oh no, sir,' he assured me, 'everything's well under control.'
'I've telephoned about . . . that concerns us both.'
'Oh . . . er . . . . Does that mean that my application for
promotion has been approved?'
'I know nothing about promotion,' I said. 'I'm referring to the
fifty pounds you borrowed from me a year ago.'
'Fifty pounds a year ago?' George repeated. 'You are Mr Marvin
Newman, . . . Headquarters, aren't you?'
'I'm Mr Martin Newnham of Norbury,' I said, 'and you'll
remember you borrowed . . . to last year's Derby.'
His tone changed again. 'Oh! Well. I'm an extremely busy man so
I haven't any time to waste,' he stated. 'You might ring at a more
convenient time. Goodbye.'

Examination practice

Reading comprehension, Section A (page 160)

1C 2D 3B 4D 5C 6C 7D 8B 9A 10C

Reading comprehension, Section B (page 162)

1D 2B 3C 4A 5B 6A

Use of English, Section A (page 163)

1 the   2 book / theoretical   3 one   4 school / academic / formal
5 is   6 to   7 little / no / insufficient   8 must / do   9 attend
10 for   11 on   12 in   13 opportunity / chance   14 up   15 their

16 with   17 countryside   18 early / surely   19 pleasure / enjoyment
20 life / oneself

Use of English, Section B (page 164)

1   The bus descended and then climbed steeply. It swerved, moved quickly along a level road and changed direction again before stopping. (*21 words*)
2   The bus had passed the forward-moving procession so that the latter was seen from behind. When the bus moved in the opposite direction, the procession was seen approaching.
3   The tanging of the church bell, the men's deep voices and the women's high voices.
4   The slope was a steep one and continued for a long way.
5   The village was already familiar enough to give the travellers a sense of ownership.
6   glitter.
7   It was compact, individuals being close to one another.
8   Both indicate something that crosses: a saddle over a horse's back and a bridge over space.
9   The italics suggest abrupt surprise.
10 The gradual decrease in speed and engine noise.
11 This construction emphasises the subject 'procession'.
12 could be heard.
13 The image weighed heavily on their shoulders.
14 At different angles.
15 It was moving along a level ridge and with steep mountain slopes and deep valleys on either side. Below at different heights of a facing slope were two villages which could be reached by a winding road. Above the procession were the grey-yellow cottages of the nearby village and ahead stood an isolated church. Brilliant sunlight created a vivid contrast between brightness and shade. (*64 words*)

General practice (page 164)

1   1 apart from   2 but   3 excluding / except   4 in contrast
    5 except   6 without   7 on the other hand   8 also   9 besides
    10 on the contrary   11 beside

2   1 They bought a small cottage . . .
    2 I can't tell you yet . . .
    3 Though apparently talkative they are people . . .
    4 He spoke so quietly . . .
    5 I saved as much money . . .
    6 She found some early purple orchids . . .
    7 She consulted the newspaper to see . . .
    8 It was the only thing . . .
    9 A higher standard of living was . . .
    10 I telephoned the neighbour . . .

3   1 Your father has been involved in an accident necessitating an emergency operation on his spine. He keeps asking for you.
    2 I regret that the match has been postponed as the pitch is waterlogged. I suggest a fixture Saturday week or when convenient later.

3 Thank you for the post offered which I accept. I can start on 1st March. I shall be writing to confirm this.

4 The consignment due yesterday has not been received. Please cancel the order if the goods have not already been despatched as they are needed urgently.

5 My landlady is angry as I have no money left. My examinations are to take place next month. Please send £100.

6 Please undertake an assignment covering the Ruritanian earthquake. You will accompany the star photographer Porlock, in a charter plane leaving London Airport at 6 p.m. today. Cover especially human interest features and relief schemes.

7 We have no key to the filing cabinet as Harper is in hospital for an emergency appendicitis operation and there is nobody in his flat. The second key is missing. Please send yours immediately. Enjoy your holiday.

8 Please extinguish the gas left burning in the kitchen and check the sitting-room window. The key is at Number 32. I had a horrible crossing.

4 1 FURNISHED FLAT wanted. Central. 1 bedroom, lounge, kitchen, bathroom. Central heating. £130 monthly maximum rent.

2 ITALIAN LESSONS given by graduate Italian national. Single pupils or groups. All levels.

3 VACATION EMPLOYMENT sought by university student. Clerical, youth work, interviewing, guiding, tutorial etc. Sociable and adaptable.

4 GOLDEN RETRIEVER PUPPY (6 months) lost on Saturday in Elm Park. Child's pet. Reward offered.

8

Reading, vocabulary and comprehension

Word distinctions (page 169)

landscape etc.

(a) view (b) landscape (c) scenery (d) scene (e) outlook
(f) sight (g) spectacle·

Viewpoint and *point of view* share the meaning of a personal way in which a question is considered, but *viewpoint* can also refer to a place from which a scene is observed.

strange etc.
(a) eerie   (b) weird   (c) inexplicable   (d) peculiar   (e) uncanny
(f) quaint   (g) queer   (h) strange   (i) odd

reveal etc.
(a) expose   (b) disclose   (c) uncover   (d) reveal   (e) publish
(f) unveil   (g) show

hide etc.
(a) hush up   (b) hide   (c) disguise   (d) cloak   (e) camouflage
(f) cover up   (g) conceal

Explaining the meaning of words and phrases (page 170)

(a) A picture with a quite different theme and arrangement can take its place immediately.
(b) It is given a cruel and frighteningly evil power of mockery.
(c) appears on top of
(d) who looks into her mirror when she is afraid and needs comfort and encouragement.
(e) Science has again directed our thoughts away from metaphysical speculations.

Short answers to questions (page 171)

1 As the person looking into the mirror alters his angle of vision, the objects as reflected in the mirror and their grouping there change at once.
2 The room itself may have many defects and discomforts but it appears idealised in its mirror picture.
3 People as portrayed in a mirror are idealised, losing the frailties and feelings of ordinary mortal creatures.
4 The breath of a living person will cause a mistiness on the mirror surface.
5 It distorts the human body so that the head, trunk or limbs are enlarged or compressed in relation to one another or repulsively misshapen.
6 The movement of the swans causes ripples and these, by distorting the smooth water surface, apparently shatter the reflections into meaningless coloured shapes, which nevertheless seem to form a pattern.
7 In the looking-glass world Alice meets various characters and has experiences which, apparently fantastic, could embody the unknown world of the subconscious.
8 Sand is one of the main components of glass and glass has some resemblance to water. The mirror is coated with mercury, the 'dancing' or moving metal.
9 Mirror reflections are only visual and have no solidity.

Longer answers to questions (page 171)

1 Although a mirror presents an unerringly exact reproduction of whatever is in front of it, what it shows and the arrangement of the objects can be transformed by a slight movement. The viewer is reproduced in the picture he sees, so that his own face, which it is impossible for him to see, is visible to

52

him and he can observe what is behind him and therefore invisible to him. The untidy world is idealised so that even its imperfections appear perfect. (*82 words*)

2 The windows of lighted carriages in trains offer the advantage of allowing the observation of other passengers without their being aware of this, but the watcher also has the unpleasant shock of suddenly recognising his own face. Spoons and taps distort objects reflected in their surfaces. Unruffled lake surfaces give an impression of serenity, even of non-existent beauty, and, when they are disturbed, can shatter and reform reflections. They may suggest an underwater world of eternal calm. (*77 words*)

3 Even in its practical uses, a mirror can suggest magic. Incorporated in a telescope it helps to concentrate light from remotest space. It may be used to distinguish between life and death. An entertainer can create illusions with mirrors. Lake reflections suggest a secret underwater world. The glass itself, formed of liquid silica and mobile metal, is mysterious. Above all, the idea of our own separate embodiment, in an idealised form, free from human defects and frailties, promotes the idea that if we could free ourselves from our bodies and the known world, we could discover a quite different type of reality from any we are normally aware of. (*109 words*)

Language practice
Grammar

Short answers in spoken English (page 171)

1 Yes, we do. (No, we don't).   2 No, they couldn't.
3 No, they aren't.   4 No, he won't.   5 Yes, I did. (No, I didn't).
6 Yes, they should.   7 No, I wouldn't.   8 No, they haven't.
9 Yes, I do. (No, I don't).   10 No, they hadn't. (Yes, they had.)
11 Yes, they must. (No, they needn't).   12 Yes, you have.

Question tags (page 172)

1 isn't it.   2 can we?   3 mayn't we.   4 oughtn't I
5 shouldn't they?   6 have they?   7 won't you.   8 wasn't he?
9 did you   10 mustn't I.   11 did he?   12 doesn't he?
13 do you?   14 didn't it.   15 doesn't he.   16 did it?
17 didn't you?   18 will you.   19 am I?

Adverbs (page 172)

1 The minimum number of words to show usage are given here.

   (a) worry unduly;   plan practically;   change fundamentally;   injure slightly;   modify substantially;   vary widely;   wash thoroughly;   take seriously;   observe strictly;   forbid absolutely.

(b) unduly nervous; practically certain; fundamentally honest;
slightly ill; substantially true; widely read; thoroughly tired;
seriously hurt; strictly true; absolutely false.

2 inordinately vain; comparatively rare; merely average; wholly
mistaken; largely correct; virtually forgotten; inherently noble;
partly understood; incredibly sensitive; essentially true.

3 His work is good on the whole. By and large people have accepted him.
Now and again he loses his temper. Broadly speaking it lasted two
hundred years.

4 Incidentally, we mustn't forget to ask about excursions. Certainly you
can come. Surely you understand now. Really, that's too thoughtless!
Actually I'd forgotten it. Eventually he'll understand it. Finally he
stormed out furious. Seriously, I think he could be a criminal.
Obviously the bus has gone. Evidently they no longer live here.
Apparently they left in a great hurry. Primarily you need a long
complete rest. Moreover she can also speak Gaelic. Nevertheless, I
think it's you who must apologise.

6 (a) substance   substantiate   substantial   substantially
(b) simplicity   simplify   simple   simply
    simplification
(c) provocation   provoke   provocative   provocatively
(d) solemnity   solemnise   solemn   solemnly
    solemnisation
(e) table   table   tabular
(f) sufficiency   suffice   sufficient   sufficiently
(g) practice   practise   practical   practically
(h) enthusiasm   enthuse   enthusiastic   enthusiastically
(i) necessity   necessitate   necessary   necessarily
(j) repulsion   repel (repulse) repellent   repellently
    repulsiveness   repulsive   repulsively
(k) finality   finalise   final   finally
(l) memory   memorise   memorable   memorably
(m) strength   strengthen   strong   strongly
(n) school   school   scholastic   scholastically
(o) system   systematise   systematic   systematically

Prepositions (page 173)

1 (Word groups only are suggested.)
He lives near. / near the house. He walked along. / along the street.
It has happened before. / before breakfast. It fell down. / down the
slope. He turned round. / round the park. It dropped through. /
through the tunnel.

2 (Word groups only are suggested.)
(a) for three months; during the interval; since Christmas; in May.
(b) between two houses; among the trees.
(c) swim in the pool; jump into the pool.

(d) stand on a chair; get up on to a chair.
(e) go out of a house; stand outside a house.
(f) a cottage beside a stream; study music besides training as an athlete
(g) through the window; throughout his life.
(h) go to the table; take a few steps towards the tiger; go up to a person to ask the way; until four o'clock.

3 (a) on   (b) in   (c) against   (d) by   (e) at, in   (f) via
   (g) with, in, with   (h) at

4 (a) due to   (b) owing to   (c) thanks to   (d) due to   (e) owing to
   (f) owing to   (g) thanks to

6 (Word groups only are suggested.)
   living apart from his parents;   nobody apart from his dog;   suffering from toothache in addition to headache;   lose money on account of the strike;   see a house with a view to buying it;   with reference to your recent letter;   succeed in spite of difficulties;   behave in accordance with the rules;   communicate by means of carrier-pigeons;   keep in touch with an old friend;   Europe with the exception of Great Britain (the Continent);   procedure in the event of an accident;   go to Sweden by way of Norway;   in search of a lost child;   a young man free of family responsibilities;   in return for past services;   succeed as a result of a lucky accident;   play football again provided that he is fit;   buy land for the purpose of building a house;   make a speech in favour of equal pay;   for use in case of fire.

Punctuation

Revision (page 174)

1 (a) The speaker had addressed my cousin. / My cousin looked at me.
   (b) He has one car. / He has more than one; this refers to one of them.
   (c) The cupboard was made of walnut. / It had panels made of walnut.
   (d) In the first sentence 'River's' is the name of a shop.
   (c) In the first sentence 'Silas Marner' is the title of a book.
   (f) 'naturally' = of course / naturally = without any show.
   (g) He drank when he was worried. / He had contracted the habit when he had been worried.
   (h) Were these the words he said? / Did he tell you who was there?
   (i) On that date / on that play.

2 (a) 'Mr Matthews, what . . . accidents?' asked the B.B.C. announcer.
   'The causes . . . groups: road . . . driving,' was the expert's reply.
   'Would . . . latter, please,' the announcer requested.
   'Yes, indeed. Careless overtaking, faulty brakes, failure . . .
   enough, lack of consideration: these I should . . . common.'
   'Is . . . accident-prone?'
   'Undoubtedly. Children's and old people's reactions can be

unpredictable. I'm . . . people also can't be careless. "The Highway Code" and, in addition, all motorists' organisations . . . concentration.'

(b) Sitting in the City of London Club, he . . . under SITUATIONS WANTED in the 'Evening Standard'. He . . . one.
'What . . . this?' he demanded. ' "Oxford graduate, ex-public-school, French and German Honours, highly . . . adaptable, widely-travelled, considerable . . . experience, interested in Politics, Economics, Psychology and Law, keen yachtsman and big-game hunter . . . abilities". Whatever . . . be?'
'Interesting,' commented his companion. 'Let me see. With . . . Home Secretary, Foreign Secretary, Chancellor of the Exchequer, Minister of Education and, of course, Prime Minister. In . . . too. Create a one-man Cabinet and . . . country. Think . . . save.'

An ex-public-school Oxford graduate with French and German Honours, who is highly intelligent and adaptable, seeks a post in which he can make use of his abilities. Besides having considerable journalistic and office experience, he is interested in Politics, Economics, Psychology and Law. He is widely-travelled and is a keen yachtsman and big-game hunter.

(c)   15 Roman Avenue(,)
                                                             Oldchester(,)
                                                             Yorks(.)

                                                             2nd September, 19-

The Manager(,)
Scholastic Books Ltd.(,)
College Street(,)
Reading(.)

Dear Sir,

Would . . . copy of 'Archaeology as a Hobby' by R. Digger, Ph.D. (publisher Mowbray Trench Ltd.).
I should . . . other of Mr Digger's books, . . . of his 'People's Guide to Roman Mosaic'.
I enclose . . . copy ordered.

                                    Yours faithfully,

                                    A. Learner

(d) He crossed the River Dee by ferry. Although . . . nine o'clock, (in June . . . country), the . . . a crimson-barred sky: its lower . . .

horizon. The small boat — 'The Golden Glen' was . . .
side — chugged . . . water. The boatman, (he was a . . . fellow),
gazed thoughtfully ahead.
    At first Donald . . . deck; then . . . locker. The past month's
experiences, which . . . him, seemed . . . incredible. The day when,
through . . . sleet, he . . . summit, the wet . . . hedge, the English
. . . watch and . . . Scotswoman . . . meal: all . . . childhood. In a
few hours' time, he would be on the London-bound express.
Mechanical noises: the . . . wheels, the train whistle, the . . . him.
    As . . . shore, where immense, shapeless tree-shadows . . . fields,
he . . . routine, of . . . him.

Choice of expression

Revision (page 176)

(b) The first paragraph only is dealt with here. Most of the faults in the
second one are similar. The numbers below refer to the sentences.

1 Absurd contrast between unnecessarily long words and somewhat
   childishly colloquial ending. Alliteration: dogged determination and
   drive; hideous holocaust. Misuse of 'holocaust'.
2 Mixed metaphors: 'shoulder to the wheel' and 'come to grips with'.
   Childish colloquialisms.
3 Emotionalism: 'stricken' and 'languishing'. A 'den' is for animals,
   and does not 'fall to bits'. Unnecessary 'really'. Contrasting
   colloquialism and abbreviated 'wasn't'
4 Cliché: 'a ministering angel'. 'Detergents' anachronistic. Mixed
   metaphor 'angel' 'armed with'. Sound of 'devoted band of
   dedicated heroines'.
5 Exaggerated metaphor followed by childish colloquialism.
   Absurdity of 'spreading healing in every direction'.
6, 7, 8 Rhetorical questions followed by absurd 'No'.
9 Cliché: 'through the length and breadth of'. Contrast between
   dramatic and colloquial. 'Decent' wrongly used. Hospitals do not
   spring up in people's paths: absurd metaphor.

Spelling aids (page 177)

1		
countries	dying	supplier
alleys	usable	delayed
curable	arrangement	bathing
dyed	skiing	alleys
fortification	measurable	unpronounceable

destroyer	bathing	died
noticeable	repaid	chimneys
awful	spied	curtseyed
remov(e)able	denial	advertisement
countrified	dyeing	politeness
reliable	spongeable	replaceable
charities	immediately	

2
brief	yield	veil
deceit	pierce	sleight
bier	sleigh	achieve
receipt	besiege	freight
neighbour	vein	heiress
reindeer	tier	conceited
piece		

Examination practice

Reading comprehension, Section A (page 182)

1A 2C 3D 4C 5C 6B 7A 8D 9D 10B

Reading comprehension, Section B (page 184)

1A 2B 3A 4C 5D 6C

Use of English, Section A (page 184)

1 1 'How do (can) I get to Rochester from here?' asked the driver.
2 He forced the chest open only to find, to his disappointment, that it was empty.
3 He fell asleep while they were discussing overwork.
4 He prefers working with his hands to working with his brain.
5 Tired as (though) she was after the party, she still washed . . . .
6 If only I were beautiful!
7 It will take about three hours to get home.
8 Peter, who is quite deaf, is said to be able to lip-read perfectly.
9 It was only after they had examined every room that the police left the house.

2 1 I would have had   2 did he have   3 think so   4 did
5 case he should   6 nor did   7 in drinking (in having)
8 the exception of

3 1 He got into conversation with the man sitting next to him.
2 Something must be done immediately about overcrowding in schools.
3 He first introduced himself and then went on to explain the purpose of his visit.
4 The Leader of the Opposition accused the Government of doing nothing . . . .

5 The Committee finally agreed to his scheme.
6 I leave it to you now to decide how . . . .
7 The least you can do is to visit him once a week.
8 He did nothing but grumble.

Use of English, Section B (page 186)

1 Both cities have extensive motor traffic and roads to cater for it.
2 The city is in a valley confined between mountain ranges to the north and south and the sea to the west.
3 The mountains to the north rise so steeply that the city ends abruptly at their foot but the mountain slopes to the south are gradual enough to allow a number of buildings to be constructed on them.
4 the assertion that Caracas has been identified with Los Angeles.
5 houses that are so scattered that they spread over a wide area which therefore provides accommodation for very few people.
6 the numbers of people are rising extremely rapidly.
7 The appearance of the town has been completely changed by the many high buildings that have been erected.
8 A rash is normally a group of spots on the human skin denoting an illness or defect in the functioning of the body. Seen from above, the scattered high buildings resemble the spots of a rash and there may be a suggestion here that they are the mark of unsatisfactory functioning in the city's growth.
9 the theory that has long been regarded as untrue that the growth of cities and other human activities are decided by the geography of the surrounding area.
10 its climate.
11 There is little land available for development between the mountain ranges and the population is increasing rapidly.
12 The location provides an ideal climate but restricts the area available for habitation.

General practice (page 187)

1 (Only the amended sentences are shown below.)
   1 They wrote regularly.
   3 She dressed in a hurry.
   5 He behaved fairly well.

2 (a) a word that is wrongly used
  (b) instructions that cannot be understood
  (c) a situation that causes worry
  (d) a demonstration that opposes war
  (e) a substance that will not burn
  (f) a factory that is no longer in use
  (g) a story that cannot be believed
  (h) an action that has not been thought about
  (i) a sky that has no clouds in it
  (j) decisions that cannot be recalled

3 (a) 1 They open the museum on Sundays.
     2 Someone shone the light in my eyes.

3 They moved the train into a siding.

4 The driver stopped the bus at 'The Swan'.

6 Mother boiled the kettle quickly.

(b) 2 This blouse washed perfectly.

3 The dinner is cooking slowly.

4 The news spread throughout the town.

6 The trains run all night.

8 The timetable changed last month.

Reading aloud (page 188)

1 The Chairman or Managing Director of a company is opening a meeting.

2 A courier is telling her coach party about arrangements for their night's stay in a hotel.

3 Someone is telling a friend about his evening at the theatre and his opinion of the show he saw.

Test papers

Reading comprehension, Section A (page 267)

1B 2A 3C 4C 5A 6A 7D 8B 9B 10C 11B 12D 13B 14A
15B 16C 17A 18D 19D 20C 21C 22B 23C 24B 25B

Reading comprehension, Section B (page 269)

First passage

1A 2B 3B 4C 5B

Second passage

1B 2A 3A 4D 5B

Third passage

1C 2A 3A 4B 5B

Use of English, Section A (page 275)

1 1 carried   2 into   3 that   4 sometimes / possibly / perhaps / occasionally   5 in   6 takes   7 on   8 sometimes / occasionally / readily / unfortunately   9 another   10 besides   11 how
12 regards   13 are   14 whose   15 conventional / established / contemporary / organised   16 on   17 while   18 robbing
19 part   20 other

2   1 Air, food and water are essential to man.
    2 'How about painting the garage green?' Mr Cinnamon suggested.
    3 The house proved to be / was much more difficult to find than we had expected.
    4 Only when he was halfway up the mountain did he realise (did he have any idea of) how difficult the climb would be.
    5 We all wanted the weather to turn cooler.
    6 You need not have carried all that shopping home yourself.
    7 She expressed her belief that he was honest (belief in his honesty / conviction that he was honest).
    8 He said that he would be having his photograph taken the next day.
    9 The deep snowdrifts made further progress impossible / blocked further progress.
    10 Mr Carroway said that it was his wife's fault that they had arrived late.

3   1 would be able   2 might have been   3 to have / supposed to have
    4 had (ever) seen   5 not go   6 not climb   7 to have been
    8 case he should

4   1 He hardly ever gets up before ten.
    2 . . . have shown much interest in preserving . . . .
    3 Would you be so kind as to move . . . .
    4 I suspect the cat from next door of having stolen the fish.
    5 Do sit down and tell me what your new house is like.
    6 We had such cold weather that we . . . .
    7 . . . Mr Clove, whose exceptional qualifications in science you drew our attention to yesterday, to the post of senior research chemist.
    8 You should make the most of your two days in Paris.
    9 The reason I am asking you about Edinburgh is that you . . . . (My reason for asking you about Edinburgh is that you . . . .)
    10 I have (full) confidence in your ability to pass the examination.

Use of English, Section B (page 278)

1   The vegetation and food which has sustained the plants and animals has come from the soil and later goes back to it.
2   A sponge soaks up and absorbs water which can be utilised later when required.
3   'our' refers to the earth's inhabitants, of whom he is one.
4   'Raw materials' are the things produced from or by the earth which are later converted into manufactured goods.
5   By the interchange of oxygen and carbon dioxide by plants and animals. The word with a similar meaning is 'thus'.
6   They would not be able to develop satisfactorily if their growth was restricted by other plants and they would not be able to get so much food from the soil.
7   The bark of trees was cut so that the trees died and other vegetation was burned.
8   This method of destroying trees and other vegetation.
9   The harvest may appear very poor in comparison with present-day standards.

10 All the nourishment has been used up so the soil is useless. 'Exhausted' can also mean 'completely tired'. A person who is completely tired has used up all his available energy.

11 The soil has been reduced to dust by over-utilisation. This dust is easily blown away by wind or washed away (especially downhill) by heavy rain.

12 The immigrants cut down the trees while primitive peoples cut their bark and left them to die.

13 In fact the commas are hardly necessary here as the expression originally used metaphorically (in the sense of 'opening a door to new possibilities') has now been absorbed into the language and does not need the commas which separate off a less common colloquial application.

14 From early times farmers made a practice of clearing the land of plants and trees in order to provide space and light for their crops. As plant food in the soil was exhausted by successive harvests, farmers abandoned that land and moved elsewhere. With no plants to retain the infertile soil, on hill-slopes and in areas of heavy rainfall especially, topsoil was washed away. When world population and accordingly food requirements were small, the soil might regain some fertility before recultivation but, with the increase of people and their needs, many areas of land lost permanently their productive capacity. (*99 words*)

Additional Practice

Vocabulary practice (page 282)

1E 2C 3B 4A 5A 6B 7D 8A 9C 10C 11E 12A 13A
14B 15D